SUFFOLK

to my wife on
my daughter's first birthday
with thanks
John

Cook Out

Cook Out

FRANCES KITCHIN

David & Charles

Newton Abbot   London   North Pomfret (Vt)   Vancouver

To my husband Ian,
who started it all by giving me my caravan
so that I can hitch up and get away from it all.

British Library Cataloguing in Publication Data

Kitchin, Frances
　　Cook out.
　　1. Cookery
　　I. Title
　　641.5　　　TX652

ISBN 0-7153-7610-1

Set in Baskerville
by HBM Typesetting Limited Chorley Lancs
and printed in Great Britain
by Biddles Limited Guildford Surrey
for David & Charles (Publishers) Limited
Brunel House Newton Abot Devon

Published in the United States of America
by David & Charles Inc
North Pomfret Vermont 05053 USA

Published in Canada
by Douglas David & Charles Limited
1875 Welch Street North Vancouver BC

Contents

Introduction

I wrote this book for the ever increasing thousands who willingly leave their homes and comfortable beds and take sheer delight in roughing it under canvas or in a caravan for a few weeks as a holiday. You might think that caravanning and camping with a tent are similar but, having done both, they are worlds apart except for cooking—usually with both one has to cook a meal on two burners and perhaps a grill. Without a guide this can lead to bacon, eggs and baked beans followed next day by the same menu or, as a change, fish and chips. This book shows how many exciting meals can be produced on limited burners with little space and equipment. The recipes are easy to follow and the results can be obtained from the novice cook; even Dad could be the 'queen of the kitchen'. The other essential ingredient besides equipment is a sense of humour and that is why this book appears, at times, to be light-hearted. Although written for campers and our friends on the water, this book would equally be at home in the bedsitter world.

I would like to thank the following for information: the English Tourist Board, the Scottish Tourist Board, the Irish Embassy, the White Fish Authority, the National Dairy Council, Ted Tuckerman—an enthusiastic angler and television colleague—and information derived by reading Richard Mabey's *Food for Free*. The other very important people I must thank are my mother, Mrs Marjorie Sherrin, another keen caravanner, who patiently corrected my spelling; my children Jacinta and Peter who did extra household chores and supplied me with endless cups of coffee while I fought my typewriter.

Frances Kitchin
Witcombe, 1977

Useful Guides to Measuring

Spoon Measuring

1 level spoon = a spoon filled just to the rim
1 heaped spoon = as much on the spoon as possible, heaped high
1 rounded spoon = as much above the rim of the spoon as below
4 level teaspoons = 1 level tablespoon
2 heaped teaspoons = 1 rounded dessertspoon

Dry Ingredients

1oz flour = 1 heaped tablespoon
1oz rice = 1 level tablespoon
1oz oatmeal = 2 heaped tablespoons
1oz granulated sugar = 1 rounded tablespoon
1oz demerara sugar = 1 level tablespoon
1oz castor sugar = 1 heaped tablespoon
1oz chopped suet = 1 heaped tablespoon
1oz currants = 1 level tablespoon
1oz soft breadcrumbs = 3 heaped tablespoons
1oz lentils = 2 level tablespoons
1oz jam or marmalade = 1 heaped dessertspoon
1oz treacle or syrup = 1 level tablespoon
1 average sized egg = 2oz; 8 eggs make 1lb (455g)

Metric Measure

Ounces	Grammes	Fluid ounces	Millilitres
1	30	5 ($\frac{1}{4}$ pint)	150
4	115	10 ($\frac{1}{2}$ pint)	275
8	225	15 ($\frac{3}{4}$ pint)	425
16 (1lb)	455 (0.5 kilos)	20 (1 pint)	575 (0.6 litres)

List of Equipment

The Very Least One Needs

Set of billies, which usually includes a lid that acts as a frying pan
Portable burner, unless a fire is used
Good sharp knife
Can opener
Matches
Water carrier which can be a plastic bottle
Personal kit of cutlery, plate and mug
Small teacloth and dishcloth
Small quantity of washing-up liquid

To Make Life a Little Easier

Small chopping board or tough plate
Small jug or basin
Small bucket or bowl
Pot scourer
Wooden spoon

Equipment for a Family Holiday in a Tent or Caravan

Aluminium foil
Two burners on a stand
Set of saucepans
Kettle
Two large bowls, for a salad or for use as a mixing bowl
Measuring jug
Cooking equipment—wooden spoon, fish slice, good knife
Water container
Bucket for liquid waste
Lighter, either matches or gas torch
Teacloths, dishcloth and pot scourer
Each member has a plate, bowl, mug, glass (if room) and cutlery
Extra luxury for the cook—grater, whisk, heavy casserole pot, colander, pressure cooker, serving platter and plastic containers
Dust pan and brush

9

Campers' Larder

This depends so much as to whether the camper has to carry every item on his back or whether he has a large boot that's got space to take the kitchen sink.

For Those Carrying All on Their Back

It's advisable to decide as far as possible just how adventuresome you expect your cooking to be. Will it be a fry-up each night or include the odd curry? You will realise that the smallest quantity that is sold over the counter is more than you will ever need and it's senseless to carry it around the countryside. An example is salt; the smallest quantity sold is too much and you'd be well advised to have a small light container and pour in enough for your needs. Another example are herbs; they add so much to the dullest stew or soup, but even the small tubs are more than a camper would need, so transform them into light 'Tic Tac' containers. Remember to label all items well.

Salt and pepper
Small quantity of flour for thickening, and for dusting before frying
Small quantity of oil, because fat will melt in the heat
Few stock cubes
Herbs and curry powder if the latter is to be used
Instant mashed potato
Packet of instant soup, which can be used as a base for fresh soups or as a gravy
Tube of tomato purée
Dried milk
Crisp breads, in case you are miles from the nearest baker
Drinks—tea, coffee, squash, etc

Having got this as one's basic larder, it's advisable to buy items when needed. Try not to over-buy as this will cause a problem when you next move. It will also mean your meals will lack variety, and there could be a danger of food poisoning.

For a Family and the Camper Who Has Plenty of Room

Most of the above applies and the cook, to some extent, should plan her menus while stocking the larder. In my caravan I carry the following, and this can be a guide, but another person's larder will vary according to the way of life that person normally leads.

Salt and pepper
Garlic salt or garlic cloves
Tomato sauce
Tomato purée in a tube
Mango chutney
Small box of stock cubes
Flour for thickening, and for dusting before frying
Small quantity of mixed herbs
Drinks—tea, coffee, squash, etc
Small can of evaporated milk and a little dried milk
Instant mashed potato
Rice and sometimes pasta
Oil
Cereals
Jam and marmalade
Butter, but only that which is in use
Tin of baked beans
Small tin of tomatoes
Biscuits and a packet of crisp bread
Packet of soup
Odd onion and garlic from my garden
Few eggs from my chickens
Washing-up liquid
Scouring powder
Small quantity of washing powder (small packets can be bought from the vending machines at launderettes)

I buy in small quantities and only renew milk, cheese, eggs, bread, fruit, vegetables etc when out or short. Also when special ingredients are needed for a dish I want to make but haven't provided for in the larder.

A Few Tips

1 When buying food buy little and often, thus saving the problem of storage.

2 Cover fish and crustaceans in cold water, preferably salted, if they are to be kept a few hours before using.

3 If possible, don't attempt to keep meat in hot weather but, if you do, wash with a solution of vinegar and water.

4 Butter and milk are best stored in the cool, covered with a cloth which has its ends resting in water.

5 Heat kills most bacteria so if in doubt boil, eg soups, for a few minutes.

6 Never place a lid on a pan when cooling for further use; bacteria is active under the lid. Better to cover with a clean cloth.

7 Keep vegetables in the cool and not in closed plastic as they sweat. Plastic bags can be used if there are ample holes.

8 Don't store hot and cold food together.

9 Keep food covered with lids, foil or clean tights.

10 Keep wine cool by leaving the bottle, with its cork intact, in a bucket of water.

11 Don't leave items of food under the caravan or beside the tent without ample protection against straying dogs.

12 If you have any doubts as to whether food has gone off take no chances and throw it away.

13 Forget deep frying while camping as it's an added risk when cooking in a small area and the cooling of the fat causes problems. Sauté potatoes are as good as chips but, if you want the real thing, buy them cooked from a fish and chip shop.

14 Make sure all cooking pans and eating utensils are well washed.

1

Breakfast Without Cereals

Admit it, most of the breakfasts eaten on sites consist of a bowl of wheaties with perhaps the addition of toast. In France the order of the day is croissants or bread with apricot preserve. I remember one remarkable breakfast that I witnessed on a site in France. A foreigner piled his plate with a large hunk of bread and then helped himself to apricot jam and topped it all with gherkins. I spread my own toast with amazement and thought he must have made some awful mistake due to his sleepiness, but was shocked when the whole family followed suit. Somehow we English are a little more conventional in our choice of breakfast. It is a good idea to have a substantial one which could be called brunch and served nearer to midday. Of course there's the traditional bacon and eggs, but why not make a change and try some of the following recipes. Who knows, you might progress to gherkins with apricot jam!

Hot Breakfast Grapefruit

Ingredients

1 grapefruit cut in half
1tbs marmalade

2tbs soft brown sugar

Method

1 Heat the grill. Spread marmalade and sprinkle sugar on each half of the grapefruit and slide under the grill.
2 Cook until hot and bubbly, serve at once.

Variations

Hot spicy grapefruit using 1 grapefruit, 2tbs soft brown sugar, ½tsp mixed spice.
Hot honey grapefruit using 1 grapefruit, 2tbs soft brown sugar, 1tbs honey.
Hot buttered grapefruit using 1 grapefruit, 2oz soft brown sugar, 1oz butter, pinch of cinnamon.
Serves 2 portions.

Quick Kedgeree

Ingredients

2 hard boiled eggs
2oz (55g) butter
4oz (115g) cooked long grain
  rice

8oz (225g) cooked smoked
  haddock
seasoning

Method

1 Chop one of the eggs and slice the other.
2 Melt the butter and sauté the rice in it for a minute, then add the chopped egg, flaked haddock and stir well over a low heat for 3 minutes. Add seasoning.
3 Pile the mixture on a serving dish and garnish with the sliced egg and parsley (if available).

Serves 4 portions.

Square Eggs

Ingredients

1 piece of bread
little oil

1 egg

Method

1 Melt oil and cook the bread in it on one side. Remove bread from the pan and make a square in its centre.
2 Return the bread to the pan with the cooked side uppermost. Drop the egg in the small square. Cook until set. Serve at once.

This method prevents the egg from spreading over the pan.

Serves 1 portion.

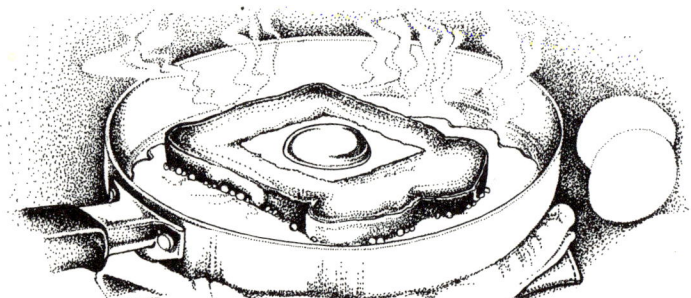

Scrambled Kipper

Ingredients

8oz (225g) cooked kipper
1oz butter or margarine
6 eggs
3tbs milk
seasoning

4 slices of buttered toast or
  fried bread
few slices of tomato for
  decoration

Method

1 Melt the butter or margarine in a pan and add the lightly beaten eggs, milk and seasoning. Mix over a low heat.
2 Mash kippers and add to the egg mixture. Cook until creamy in texture.
3 Pile on the bread and decorate with the sliced tomato.
Serves 4 portions.

Bacon Scramble

As above but substitute 4oz of crispy bacon instead of the kipper.

Cottage Cheese Scramble

Ingredients

1oz butter or margarine
3tbs milk
seasoning
pinch of garlic salt

6 eggs
4oz (115g) cottage cheese
4 slices buttered toast

Method

1 Melt butter with the milk. Add seasoning and beaten eggs.
2 Cook until the mixture begins to thicken, then add the cottage cheese. Cook for a few minutes until mixture is soft.
3 Serve at once on buttered toast.
Serves 4 portions.

Cornbeef Hash

Ingredients

oil for frying
1 large onion
8oz (225g) tin of cornbeef

4oz (115g) cooked potato or
  instant potato
seasoning

Method
1 Melt oil and fry the onion.
2 Mash the cornbeef with the potato and seasoning, and add to the onion.
3 Stir-fry until piping hot and serve straight from the pan with a fried egg.

Serves 4 portions.

Omelettes

Basic recipe for a plain omelette

To each egg add ¼oz butter or margarine, 1tsp water, pinch of salt and pepper (if sweet ¼tsp sugar).
1 Melt the butter or margarine in a flat pan and heat slowly, not allowing to brown.
2 In a bowl lightly whisk the egg with the water and seasoning.
3 Pour the egg mixture into the pan and allow to settle. Then with a fork keep the mixture moving but do not stir or you will get scrambled egg, and not a fluffy consistency.
4 When the mixture looks set, loosen the edges and tilt the pan away from you and fold the omelette in half. Serve upside down on a warm plate.

If a filled omelette is being made, the hot filling is laid on half the omelette before it is folded over.

Suggestions for fillings:

Asparagus with a little chopped parsley and a knob of butter.
Cheese—to each 2 eggs add 1oz grated cheese and seasoning.
Ham—to each 2 eggs add 1oz chopped ham and a little grated onion.
Kidney—to each 2 eggs add 1 sheep's kidney, cored and finely chopped. Sauté in a little butter.
Mixed herb omelette—to each 2 eggs add ¼tsp mixed chopped herbs before cooking.

Mushroom—if using field mushrooms, sauté in a little butter first, otherwise chop finely and use; 1tbs cream makes a creamy sauce.

Tomatoes—skin the tomatoes and remove some of the pips, otherwise just chop and add.

Jam—1tbs jam and omit salt and pepper.

Honey—treat in the same way as jam.

Spanish Omelette

Use the basic recipe but also add

1 tomato, sliced	cayenne pepper
1 small onion, sliced	pinch of herbs
1tsp oil	

Method

1 Fry the vegetables in the oil, add the pepper, herbs, egg mixture and continue as for a plain omelette.

Often Spanish omelettes are of several flavours piled on top of each other and not folded over, or built up with fillings between each omelette layer. The whole is sliced when serving.

Egg Nog

Ingredients

1 egg	little sherry, brandy, nutmeg
¼pt (150ml) milk	or vanilla essence
1tsp sugar	

Method

1 Beat egg, milk and sugar together until all traces of ropiness has gone. Strain.

2 Add the required flavouring and drink at once.

Coffee in a Jug

Ingredients

2oz (55g) ground coffee   1pt (575ml) boiling water
pinch of salt

Method

1 Place the coffee and salt in a jug and pour on the boiling water. Allow to stand for 5 to 8 minutes.
2 Drain and reheat the coffee if necessary, but do not boil.

Nightcap Coffee

Use method above but also include a tablespoon of cocoa.

Nutty Coffee

Make the coffee and serve in individual cups.
Float cream on top by pouring it slowly over the back of a spoon. Sprinkle nutmeg on top. The aroma is well worth the trouble it takes.

2

Main Courses When You Could Eat a Horse

It often amazes me how many campers will insist on having their usual meal of meat and two veg while on a site. If you have two burners, this meal is as easy while camping as it would be at home. If you have only one burner, it could cause a problem. The secret is to cook the pot that needs the longest cooking time first and try and keep it warm while cooking the other pot. Then when the second pot is cooked, just re-heat the first. If you can cook two vegetables together this will save time. Not all main meals mean meat and two veg, so I am giving you recipes for various dishes that only need rice as an accompaniment but which still make a main meal. Chapter 3 also contains many hearty meals.

One of the problems when cooking meat is to choose the correct cut, as the cheaper, tougher cuts are not suitable unless you are prepared to wait until they are cooked. Often you may have to buy meat from the camp site's deep freeze and the label only states 'stewing steak' and gives no indication of the cut. If at all possible buy fresh meat a few hours before you need it and seek the advice of the butcher. The following list gives the best cuts of meat for the camper and the best way to cook them.

For Grilling, Frying or Braising

Chops and Cutlets Can be grilled, fried or braised. They should be cooked very slowly depending on their thickness. They can be cooked in a frozen state but will need much longer over a gentle heat; check they are cooked throughout. Special care must be taken when cooking pork. By adding a sauce to the chops one can make an ordinary chop into an exciting dish.

Steaks Fillet, rump, sirloin, chateaubriand, entrecôte, tournedos, porterhouse. They are best grilled but can be fried or even braised.

Gammon Grilled or fried and garnished with pineapple.

Kidneys Fried or braised. Can be grilled if first brushed with a little oil.

Liver Grilled, fried or braised.

Black pudding Fried or grilled in slices.

Chicken Cook very slowly by braising, grilling or frying in portions, but better removed from the bone.

For Stewing

Beef Chuck, clod (sticking or neck), skirt.

Lamb Middle neck cutlets, middle neck, scrag end of neck.

Pork Belly, knuckle, spare rib.

For Boiling

Bacon joints, brisket and silverside.

To Braise Meat

The usual way to braise meat is first to brown it in a little fat and then remove it from the pot. Next brown a few chopped vegetables in the remaining fat and replace the meat on this bed of vegetables. Add a small quantity of liquid and cover with a well-fitting lid. Cook according to cut of meat, but beef will take about 2 hours; lamb will take $1\frac{1}{2}$ hours.

Ingredients

2lb flank topside
2tbs oil
12oz (340g) mixed chopped vegetables, onion, carrot, etc

pinch of herbs
seasoning
little stock or water

Method

1 Wipe the meat well and brown in the hot fat in a saucepan.
2 When the meat is well done remove it and keep it warm. Add the vegetables to the pan and brown. (There must be 2in (5cm) of vegetables on the base of the pan; if necessary add more than the 12oz depending on size of the pot.)
3 If there is a lot of grease, remove some of it. Replace the meat, add herbs and seasoning and enough water or stock to cover the vegetables but not to reach the meat.
4 Cover the pot with a well-fitting lid. If you are in doubt place a heavy tin on top.
5 Halfway through cooking time turn the meat in order to brown the top.
6 Cooking time is approximately 2 hours. Remove the meat and place on a dish ready for carving. The vegetables can be served on the dish with the meat but are best incorporated with the gravy.

Serves 8 portions.

Pot Roasting

Very similar to braising in that one cooks a joint of meat in a saucepan. Brown the joint in a little fat and then remove. Place a trivet or wire rack in the pan and replace the meat resting on it. Add a little water to the pot and cover tightly. Turn meat occasionally. Cooking time will depend on the meat. Beef and mutton take 45 minutes per lb; pork, 50 minutes per lb.

Simple Stew

Ingredients

1lb (455g) stewing steak
1 tbs oil
little swede or turnip
1 onion

2 carrots
1oz (30g) flour
seasoning
$\frac{3}{4}$pt (425ml) beef stock

Method

1 Cut the meat into 1in (2.5cm) cubes, removing excess fat and all gristle.
2 Heat the oil and fry the meat until brown. Add the chopped vegetables and cook for a few more minutes.
3 Sprinkle on the flour and cook for a minute, stirring well. Add the seasoning and pour in the stock.
4 Bring the stew to the boil and cook for 2 hours (depending on cut of meat you use), stirring frequently.
NB   The pot must have a well-fitting lid otherwise keep topping it up with liquid.

If you wish, 30 minutes before the end of the cooking time you may add some small potatoes, but see there is some liquid in which to cook them.

Serves 4 portions.

Peppered Steak with Noisette Butter

Ingredients

4 steaks (sirloin, minute or
  fillet)
2tbs oil

good shake of milled black
  pepper
2oz (55g) butter
juice of ½ lemon

Method

1 Brush the steaks with oil and shake the pepper on them. Leave
for 1 to 2 hours if possible.
2 Heat a pan and dry-fry the steaks in it. If using a grill, heat it
well before commencing cooking.
3 After the steaks are cooked, remove them and keep them hot.
Add the butter to the juices in the pan and, when the butter
starts to brown, add the lemon juice. While it's still foaming,
pour over the steaks.
Serves 4 portions.

Steak Maître d'Hôtel (with Parsley Butter)

Ingredients

2 steaks (sirloin, minute or
  fillet)
2oz (55g) butter
2tsp lemon juice

little grated lemon rind
1tbs chopped parsley
seasoning

Method

1 Soften the butter and mix in lemon juice and rind, parsley and
seasoning. Allow to set.
2 Place a good knob of the butter on the hot cooked steaks.
Serves 2 portions.

Steak Béarnaise

Ingredients

2 steaks (sirloin, minute or
  fillet)
3tbs wine vinegar
6 peppercorns
1 bayleaf

small onion
2 egg yolks
seasoning
4oz (115g) butter

Method

1 Place the vinegar, peppercorns, bayleaf and onion in a saucepan and boil until it's reduced to 1 tablespoon.
2 Mix the yolks with the seasoning and pour the vinegar mixture on them, stirring well. Add 1oz of the butter.
3 Place the bowl over hot water and cook until the mixture thickens. (It can be done directly over the heat, but care must be taken.)
4 When the sauce is thickened, add the remaining butter in small pieces.
5 Pour the sauce over the cooked steaks.

Serves 2 portions.

Homemade Beefburgers

Ingredients

1lb (455g) minced steak
1 onion
oil for frying
1tbs flour

pinch of herbs
1 egg yolk
seasoning

Method

1 Fry the finely chopped onion in a little oil and add to the minced steak.
2 Mix the flour, herbs, seasoning and yolk with the steak mixture; make into small rounds and flatten. If sticky, add a little dusting of flour.
3 Heat the remaining oil and gently fry the burgers on each side. Drain off excessive oil.

Makes approximately 14, depending on size.

Boiled Beef and Carrots

Ingredients

3lb (1.4kg) silverside of beef
3 to 4 small onions

4 to 5 carrots
seasoning

Dumplings:
8oz (225g) self-raising flour
5oz (140g) suet

good pinch of salt
little water

Method

1 Place the meat in a saucepan, add the seasoning and cover with water. Bring to the boil and remove scum.
2 Cover the pan and allow it to boil for 40 minutes. Add the onions and carrots and continue to cook for another 15 minutes.
3 Make the dumplings by mixing all the dry ingredients together and adding a little water to make a stiff dough. Divide the mixture into walnut-sized balls and drop into the pan. Continue to cook for 20 minutes.
4 To serve, remove the beef from the gravy and surround it with the drained vegetables and dumplings. The gravy, if desired, can be served separately.

Serves 8 portions.

Hot Boiled Bacon Joint

Ingredients

2lb (1kg) boiling joint of bacon
1 bayleaf

8 even sized carrots

Method

1 Place the bacon in a large pan and fill with water. Add the bayleaf, cover and bring it to the boil.
2 Half an hour before the cooking time has been completed add the carrots. Cook altogether for 1 hour.
3 Drain the bacon joint well, remove the rind (if any), and brush the outside of the fat with breadcrumbs. It is then ready to carve. Serve the carrots separately.
4 A parsley sauce is very good served with a bacon joint.

Serves 4 portions.

Beef Stroganoff

Ingredients

8oz (225g) fillet or rump steak
1oz (30g) butter
1 chopped onion
4oz (115g) sliced mushrooms
freshly milled black pepper

small carton of sour cream
4–6oz (115–175g) hot
  cooked Patna rice as
  accompaniment

Method

1 Cut the steak into very thin strips.
2 Melt the butter and cook the onion and mushrooms. Drain and keep warm.
3 Fry the meat in remaining butter for 10 to 15 minutes. Replace the onion and mushrooms and season well.
4 Lower the heat and stir in the sour cream and warm through but *do not let it boil*. Serve with warm rice.

Serves 2 portions.

Beef Curry

Ingredients

1lb (455g) stewing steak
2tbs oil
1 large onion
1tbs flour
2tbs curry powder
½pt (300ml) beef stock

salt
1 cooking apple
1tbs tomato purée
6–8oz (175–225g) cooked
  Patna rice

Method

1 Cube the meat and fry it in the oil. Add the chopped onion and cook until golden.
2 Stir in the flour and curry powder and cook for 1 minute. Add the chopped apple.
3 Stir in the tomato purée and pour on the stock. Seasoning to taste with the salt.
4 Cook for 30 to 45 minutes depending on cut of meat.
5 Serve separately from the rice. Also serve a few accompaniments with the curry, eg mango chutney, cucumber in sour cream, bananas, desiccated coconut, sliced tomato, etc.

Serves 4 portions.

Jambalaya

Ingredients

1tbs oil
1oz (30g) butter
1 onion
1 clove of garlic
8oz (225g) cooked ham or pieces
8oz (225g) prawns
small tin tomatoes

salt
$\frac{1}{4}$tsp oregano
$\frac{1}{4}$tsp thyme
few drops tabasco sauce (or good pinch of cayenne)
$\frac{1}{4}$pt (150ml) white wine
6oz (170g) Patna rice

Method

1 Heat the oil and butter together and sauté the sliced onion and crushed garlic.
2 Stir in the chopped ham, prawns, tomatoes, seasoning, herbs, rice and wine.
3 Cover the pot with a lid, bring to the boil and simmer for 30 minutes until all the liquid has been absorbed or rice is cooked. If the rice is not cooked, add more liquid and cook a little longer.

Serves 4 portions.

Lamb Risotto

Ingredients

1lb (455g) lamb, either leg or shoulder
4tbs oil
1pt (575ml) beef stock
1 onion

1 clove of garlic
4oz (115g) sliced mushrooms
seasoning
4oz (115g) Patna rice

Method

1 Cut the lamb into small cubes and fry in 2tbs of oil until brown. Add the stock and cook covered for 20 minutes.
2 Fry the onion and garlic in remaining oil and add to the lamb. Slice the mushrooms and add to the lamb mixture with seasoning.
3 Sprinkle in the rice, bring saucepan to the boil, and simmer for 20 minutes until rice has absorbed the liquid and is tender.

Serves 4 portions.

Spaghetti Bolognaise

Ingredients

1 onion
1 clove of garlic
1tbs oil
1lb (455g) minced beef
seasoning
pinch of herbs

1tbs tomato purée
small tin of tomatoes
1tbs flour
½pt (275ml) beef stock
1lb (455g) spaghetti

Method

1 Fry the chopped onion and crushed garlic in the oil. Add the meat and cook until brown.
2 Add the seasoning, herbs, purée and tomatoes, and allow to cook for 10 minutes.
3 Sprinkle on the flour, mixing it in well and add the stock. Cook for 20 to 30 minutes, stirring often.
4 Cook the spaghetti separately as directed on the packet and toss it in butter.
5 Serve the sauce with the spaghetti and sprinkle on some parmesan cheese.

Serves 4 portions.

Liver with Apples

Ingredients

8 slices of calf's liver
2tbs flour
2tbs oil
2oz (55g) butter
2 cooking apples, cut into rings

2tbs brandy
2tbs lemon juice
½ a chicken cube mixed in
⅛pt (75ml) of water

Method

1 Sprinkle the liver with the flour and cook in the oil. Drain and keep warm.
2 Melt the butter and fry the apple rings in it until soft, then remove and keep warm. Add the brandy, stock and lemon juice and reduce a little.
3 Pour the sauce over the liver and decorate with the apple rings.

Serves 4 portions.

Very Quick Chilli Con Carne

Ingredients

1 onion
1oz (30g) butter
1lb (455g) minced beef
1tbs tomato purée
11oz (312g) can of tomatoes
3tsps chilli powder

16oz (455g) can of red
  kidney beans (if not
  available use baked beans)
1 beef cube
salt
4–6oz (115–175g) cooked
  Patna rice

Method

1 Fry the chopped onion in the butter, add the meat and cook until browned.
2 Stir in the rest of the ingredients and allow to simmer for 30 minutes.
3 Serve with boiled rice.
This dish could be made with tinned minced meat to lessen the cooking time.
Serves 4 portions.

Boozy Rabbit (or Chicken)

Ingredients

4tbs oil
1 rabbit or chicken cut into
  pieces
2oz (55g) chopped bacon
2 sliced onions
1lb (455g) fresh or tinned
  tomatoes

½pt (275ml) cider
pinch of herbs
1 bayleaf
1tsp sugar
seasoning

Method

1 Heat the oil and fry the meat and onions until golden.
2 Add the rest of the ingredients and bring to the boil. Cook for 20 minutes. Remove the bayleaf and serve with vegetables.
Serves 4 portions.

Tripe and Onions

Ingredients

1½lb (670g) cleaned blanched
tripe
1lb (455g) onions, sliced
1½pt (0.8l) milk

1 bayleaf
pinch of nutmeg
seasoning

Method

1 Cut the tripe into 2in (5cm) squares. Place in water and bring to the boil.
2 Drain tripe and throw away the water. Return tripe to the saucepan and add the sliced onions, milk and seasonings. There must be enough milk to cover the tripe.
3 Simmer for 1 hour until the tripe is soft and tender. Remove the bayleaf before serving.

If the sauce is too thin, thicken with a little flour mixed in cold water.

3

At Sixes and Sevens

A meal that is served in the late afternoon or early evening could be called 'high tea'. This to me is a substantial snack eaten with a knife and fork and followed by bread and cakes, though no doubt Northerners might argue with my definition of the term. If you want a more complete meal then refer to Chapter 2. I suppose to most campers this evening meal is the most important one of the day, which has often been spent moving from one site to another or away from base.

Eggs make a good nutritious and easy snack as they can be either scrambled, fried, poached or made into omelettes. Another good standby is baked beans on toast. In this chapter I hope to give you a few more ideas and, when the family rush around shouting 'I'm starving' you, at least, won't be at sixes and sevens.

Potato Rounds

Ingredients

1lb (455g) mashed potato or use instant potato	seasoning
	little flour for dusting
1 egg yolk	4tbs oil
4oz (115g) cooked chopped bacon	

Method

1 Make sure the potato is on the dry side before adding the yolk, bacon and seasoning.
2 Sprinkle the flour on a board or plate and make the mixture into 6 flat rounds approximately ½in (1.2cm) thick.
3 Heat the oil and fry the rounds in it until golden. Drain and serve.

Serves 3 to 4 portions.

Crispy Tuna Pie

Ingredients

1 tin tuna fish
½pt (275ml) mushroom sauce
or a small tin of condensed
soup

2pkts plain crisps

Method

1 Make the sauce or heat the soup and fold in the drained tuna fish. Place in a container.
2 Sprinkle the crisps on top and serve.
Serves 2 to 3 portions.

Liver and Savoury Rice

Ingredients

2oz (55g) butter
8oz (225g) lamb's liver
2oz (55g) long grained rice
1 small green pepper
1 small onion

2oz (55g) mushrooms
2 tomatoes
4tbs white wine or stock
2tbs cream or top of milk
seasoning

Method

1 Melt 1oz of the butter in a pan and add the finely sliced liver. Cook until tender.
2 Cook the rice in salted water and drain well.
3 Chop the pepper, onion, mushrooms and tomatoes and sauté in the remaining butter. When cooked add rice and stir well, then place the mixture on a serving dish.
4 Add the wine or stock to the liver and heat, then add the cream and warm through.
5 Pour the liver mixture on top of the rice and serve at once.
Serves 4 portions.

Boston Pie

Ingredients

1 small onion, finely chopped
8oz (225g) sausages
1 large can of baked beans
1 tbs sugar

1 tbs vinegar
8oz (225g) mashed or
    instant potato

Method

1 Fry the onion and chopped sausages in a little fat until golden. Place in a serving dish.
2 Heat the baked beans with the sugar and vinegar, and place on top of the sausages.
3 Make up the instant potato, heat it (or mashed potato) well and place on top of the beans. Serve at once.

Serves 3 to 4 portions.

Chicken Risotto

Ingredients

1oz (30g) butter
1 onion, finely chopped
4oz (115g) chopped bacon
2 large cooked chicken portions
4oz (115g) sliced mushrooms

$\frac{1}{2}$ green pepper (sliced and
    seeded)
seasoning
1pt (575ml) chicken stock
8oz (225g) long grain rice

Method

1 Melt the butter and fry onion and bacon until brown.
2 Skin and chop chicken into very small pieces and add to the bacon mixture.
3 Place the bacon mixture, mushrooms, green pepper, seasoning and stock in a large pan. Sprinkle in the rice.
4 Cook the mixture over a low heat for 20 to 30 minutes, giving it the odd careful stir until all the liquid has been absorbed and rice is cooked.

This can be served from the pan or placed on a serving dish and garnished with sliced uncooked tomato and parsley.

Serves 4 portions.

Sweet Sour Porkies

Ingredients
- 1oz (30g) butter
- 1 onion, finely chopped
- 8oz (225g) sausages
- 8oz (225g) long grain rice

Sauce:
- 1tbs sugar
- 2tbs vinegar
- 1tbs cornflour
- 1tbs soy sauce
- $\frac{1}{4}$pt (150ml) water
- 1tbs tomato purée

Method
1 Heat the butter and fry the onion and chopped sausages until very crisp. Keep warm.
2 Cook the rice and drain well.
3 Mix all the sauce ingredients together, bring to the boil and cook until it thickens.
4 Place the rice on a serving dish, then the sausages and finally pour over the sauce. Serve at once.
Serves 4 portions.

Chicken and Sausage Pilaff

Ingredients
- 2oz (55g) butter or oil
- 1 large onion, chopped
- 8oz (225g) long grain rice
- 1pt (575ml) chicken stock

- seasoning
- 4oz (115g) cooked chicken
- 2oz (55g) raisins or sultanas
- 1lb (455g) sausages

Method
1 Melt half the butter or oil, fry the onions until golden and add the rice.
2 Add the stock and seasoning, bring to the boil and simmer carefully for 20 minutes until rice is cooked and liquid has been absorbed.
3 When rice is cooked add the cubed chicken and fruit and heat well.
4 Fry the whole sausages in the remaining butter until crisp.
5 Pile the pilaff on a serving dish and stand the sausages around it.
Serves 4 portions.

Kidneys with Orange

Ingredients

4oz (115g) shaped pasta	1 level tbs flour
4 lamb's kidneys	seasoning
1 small onion	1tbs tomato purée
2oz (55g) butter	6–8tbs beef stock made
1 large orange	from 1 cube

Method

1 Cook the pasta, rinse, drain and keep warm.
2 Remove skin from the kidneys, core them and chop them into small pieces. Chop the onion finely and sauté both in the melted butter.
3 When the kidneys are cooked add the finely grated rind and juice of the orange.
4 Sprinkle the flour over the mixture and cook for a few minutes, then add the seasoning, purée and stock and bring to the boil, stirring well.
5 Place the pasta on a serving dish and pour the kidney mixture on top.

It looks very nice if garnished with slices of orange and chopped parsley.

Serves 4 portions.

Curried Eggs

Ingredients

4 hot hard-boiled eggs
1 tbs oil
1 small onion
1 tbs curry powder
1 tbs flour

little salt
1 tsp tomato purée
½pt (275ml) chicken stock
8oz (225g) long grain rice

Method

1 Keep the eggs hot in a little water.
2 Make the sauce by melting the oil and frying the very finely chopped onion in it.
3 Add the curry powder and flour and cook for a few minutes. Add the salt, tomato purée and stock to the mixture. Bring to the boil while stirring.
4 Cook the rice and drain well.
5 Shell the eggs and cut in half.
6 Place the rice on a serving dish, place the eggs face downwards (on top) and pour over the sauce.

Serves 4 portions.

Savoury Mince

Ingredients

4 slices of fried bread
1 tbs oil
1 onion
1lb (455g) minced beef
1 dessertspoon flour

¼pt (150ml) water
1 beef stock cube
1 small can of tomatoes
pinch of herbs
seasoning

Method

1 Fry the finely chopped onion in the oil until crisp and then add the mince. Cook for 5 minutes.
2 Sprinkle on the flour and cook again for a few minutes, then add the water, stock cube, tomatoes, herbs and seasoning and continue to cook for 20 minutes.
3 Place the mixture in a deep serving dish. Cut the fried bread into triangles and place around the mixture.

Serves 4 portions.

Creamed Mushrooms on Toast or Fried Bread

Ingredients

1 piece of bread either toasted
  and lightly buttered, or
  fried
1oz (30g) butter

2oz (55g) mushrooms
2tbs cream or top of milk
seasoning

Method

1 Melt the butter and sauté the chopped mushrooms in it. When they are cooked pour in the cream and cook for a few more minutes. Check the seasoning.
2 Serve on the buttered toast or fried bread.

Serves 1 portion.

Egg and Onion Supreme

Ingredients

2oz (55g) butter
6oz (170g) onion
2oz (55g) flour
1pt (575ml) milk
seasoning
pinch of nutmeg

2 hard-boiled eggs
2tbs cream or top of the milk
little chopped parsley
4–6oz (115–175g) Patna
  rice or pasta

Method

1 Chop the onion very finely and brown in the butter. Add the flour and cook for a few minutes.
2 Take off the heat, then gradually add the milk. Season with the salt, pepper and nutmeg and return to heat and cook until it thickens.
3 Add the chopped eggs to the mixture and warm thoroughly. Off the heat stir in the cream. Serve garnished with the parsley, either on rice or pasta.

Serves 2 portions.

French Onion Soup

Ingredients

1 tbs oil
1 oz (30g) butter
1 lb (455g) finely chopped
  onions

1 tbs flour
1¼pt (0.7l) chicken stock
seasoning

Method

1 Melt the oil and butter together and fry the onions until light brown in colour. This is important and takes 10 to 15 minutes.
2 Add the flour and cook for a minute. Add the stock and cook for a further 20 minutes, stirring often. Check the seasoning.
3 Cut the fried bread into ½in (1.2cm) pieces.
4 Ladle the soup into heat resistant dishes and place the croutes on top. Sprinkle on the cheese and, if you have a grill, slide it under until bubbly.

NB This soup is a meal in itself and obviously better if the cheese can be grilled before serving.
Serves 2 portions.

If you are camping without an oven there are very few cakes you can make, but here are two that are easy and only need a thick-bottomed pan.

Welsh Cakes

Ingredients

6oz (170g) self-raising flour	3oz (85g) lard
3tbs fine sugar	1 egg
2oz (55g) currants	little fat for frying
pinch of nutmeg	castor sugar for dredging
pinch of salt	

Method

1 Mix all dry ingredients together, rub in the lard, and mix with the egg to a dough; add a little milk if too stiff.
2 Roll out to ¼in (0.6cm) thickness and cut into rounds.
3 Heat the pan until hot and melt a little fat in it. Place the Welsh cakes in the pan and cook slowly until dry on the outside. Turn and cook the other side.
4 Keep warm by covering with a cloth, and serve warm dredged in castor sugar.

Drop Scones

Ingredients

8oz (225g) flour	pinch of salt
½tsp bicarbonate of soda	2eggs
½tsp cream of tartar	½pt (275m) milk
3oz (85g) castor sugar	little oil for frying

Method

1 Mix flour with the other dry ingredients. Make a well in the centre and drop in the egg. Add the milk gradually to a consistency of thick cream.
2 Melt the oil and pour a little mixture in the pan and allow to cook until surface is bubbly. Turn and cook the other side; this will take approximately 4 to 6 minutes.
3 Keep warm in a cloth before serving.
Makes about 18 scones, depending on size.

Cheese Fondue

Ingredients

1 small clove garlic
¼pt (150ml) dry white wine
1tbs lemon juice
4oz (115g) grated tasty
   Cheddar or Gouda cheese

1 level tsp cornflour
seasoning
pinch of nutmeg
Loaf of crusty French bread
   cut into small cubes

Method

1 Rub the inside of an ovenproof dish or saucepan with the garlic and leave the remainder in the pan.

2 Pour in the wine and lemon juice and heat while gradually adding the cheese. Stir well and sprinkle on the cornflour, nutmeg and seasoning and cook until smooth.

3 When bubbling hot it is ready for use, and can be eaten from the pot over a low heat by each person dipping chunks of bread into the fondue with their own forks.

Serves 4 persons.

4

Afters, Puds and Posh Sweets

If I'm really honest I suppose most campers don't bother with making a sweet when fresh fruit is so available. It's so much easier to give the kids an apple than to toil over a gorgeous sweet. I adore my afters, puds or sweets, or whatever you prefer to call this course. I have a habit of judging my favourite restaurant by its sweet trolley so there must be many cooks who, like me, will take the trouble to make a gorgeous sweet to follow an easy first course.

I have purposely omitted sweets that need a sponge or pastry base because although they are easy to make at home they are impossible without an oven on a site, unless you buy a ready-made base. Meringues can be made at home and keep very well in an airtight tin, but don't bother with them unless you have plenty of room, as they can be a nightmare since they're so fragile.

Even if you are tempted to buy a convenience packet of whisk, add a little fresh fruit to it and sprinkle a few nuts on top as this makes all the difference and looks as if you have tried to make an ordinary pud into a posh sweet.

Apple Snow

Ingredients

8oz (225g) sweetened apple purée
1 stiffly beaten egg white

few sugar strains or other decoration

Method

1 Fold the egg white very carefully into the apple purée and allow it to settle for a few minutes before decorating and eating.

NB This recipe is easy but so worth while making. You can buy apple purée either dried or in little baby jars. To make it yourself you will need to chop 1lb (455g) of cooking apples and place them with very little water in a pan. Cook until tender and add the sugar. Sieve or mill the mixture and allow to cool.
Serves 2 portions.

Chocolate Cream Mousse

Ingredients
4oz (115g) plain cooking
chocolate
4 eggs, separated

1tbs castor sugar
4oz (115g) double cream

Method
1 Melt the chocolate in a bowl over a pan of hot water, then add yolks and sugar.
2 Whisk the cream until it stiffens and add to the cooled mixture. Whisk the egg whites until stiff, add 1 tablespoon to the mixture and stir it in well.
3 Fold the remaining whites into the mixture and allow to cool and set. Can be served in individual dishes but this is not necessary.
Serves 4 portions.

Crystallised Oranges

Ingredients
1 peeled fresh orange
3oz (85g) granulated sugar

$\frac{1}{4}$pt (150ml) water

Method
1 Slice the orange and place in a heat-proof container.
2 Melt the sugar in the water; simmer at first until all the sugar has dissolved and then boil rapidly until it is a golden colour.
3 Pour the sugar mixture over the orange and it will set hard in a few minutes and be ready for serving.
Serves 1 portion.

Apple Tansy

Ingredients

1lb (455g) cooking apples
2oz (55g) butter
sugar to sweeten

4oz (115g) double cream
1 egg yolk

Method

1 Peel, core and finely slice the apples. Melt the butter in a heavy pan and add the apples and a little water. Cook until soft.
2 Stir the sugar into the mixture and allow it to cool.
3 Beat the cream until stiff and add, with the yolk, to the apple mixture. Mix well.

NB This is a very old recipe and the dish can be eaten warm or chilled and is delicious with whipped cream and fruit.

Serves 4 portions.

Peach Mousse

Ingredients

1 orange jelly
small tin evaporated milk

16oz (455g) tin of peaches
4oz (115g) double cream

Method

1 Make the jelly to the instructions on the packet, but only add ¾pt (425ml) of water.
2 Whisk the evaporated milk until it stiffens and add the cooled jelly.
3 Reserve some of the peaches for decoration but chop the rest and add to the jellied mixture.
4 When the mixture has set decorate with the peaches and cream.

Serves 4 portions.

Apple Crunch Pie

Ingredients

1lb (455g) sweetened apple
  purée
quarter of a large loaf of
  bread
2oz (55g) butter

2tbs brown sugar
pinch of cinnamon
1oz (30g) plain chocolate
4oz (115g) double cream

Method

1 Make the purée and allow to cool (see method for Apple Snow, page 41).
2 Crumble the bread into crumbs. Melt the butter and fry the crumbs until crisp, then add the sugar and cinnamon.
3 Press the crumb mixture into a serving dish and allow to cool and harden.
4 Place the apple purée on top. Decorate with the grated chocolate and cream.

Serves 4 portions.

Banana Cream Syllabub

Ingredients

3 ripe bananas
1oz (30g) castor sugar
2tbs white wine

1tbs lemon juice
8oz (225g) double cream

Method

1 Peel the bananas and mash well with the sugar, wine and lemon juice.
2 Whisk the cream until stiff and fold into the mixture.
3 If possible chill before serving.

Serves 4 portions.

Royal Trifle

Ingredients

1 jam Swiss roll or some
  sponge cakes with a little jam
good wineglassful of sherry
½pt (275ml) made custard
4oz (115g) double cream

2 drops ratafia or almond
  essence (optional)
few cherries, blanched
  almonds and strips of
  angelica to decorate

Method

1 Place the sliced sponge in a dish and soak with the sherry; add
a little water if it looks too dry.
2 Pour the cooled custard over the sponge.
3 Whisk or stir the cream until stiff and add the flavourings.
4 Place the cream on top of the cold custard and decorate with
the cherries, almonds and angelica.
NB If you wanted a fluffy cream, add a stiffly beaten egg white
to the cream.
Serves 4 portions.

Jellied Trifle

Ingredients

1 jam Swiss roll
1 red jelly
small tin peaches or other
  fruit

½pt (275ml) made custard
4oz (115g) double cream
few blanched almonds and
  cherries

Method

1 Slice the Swiss roll and place in a dish.
2 Make the jelly using only ¾pt (425ml) of water. Allow to cool.
3 Place the chopped fruit on top of the sponge but keep a few
pieces back for decoration.
4 Pour cooled jelly on top of fruit and, when set, pour on the
cooled custard.
5 Whisk the cream until stiff and spread or pipe on top of cold
custard.
6 Decorate with the remaining fruit, almonds and cherries.
Serves 4 portions.

Gelatine Cheese Cake

Ingredients

2oz (55g) butter
4oz (115g) digestive biscuits

1tbs brown sugar
pinch of cinnamon

Filling:
2 eggs
6oz (170g) cream cheese
1tbs sugar
½oz (15g) gelatine

3tbs hot water
fruit, eg raspberries, black-
 currants, peaches, etc.

Method

1 Melt the butter in a pan and add the crushed digestive biscuits, brown sugar and cinnamon. Mix well and place in a serving dish. Allow to cool.

2 Separate the eggs. Mix the yolks with the cheese and sugar.

3 Dissolve the gelatine in the hot water and let it cool. From a height pour it into the cheese mixture.

4 Whisk the egg whites and carefully fold into the cheese mixture.

5 Place the fruit on top of the base, keeping a little back for decoration.

6 Spread the cheese mixture on top of fruit and decorate with remaining fruit.

Serves 4 portions.

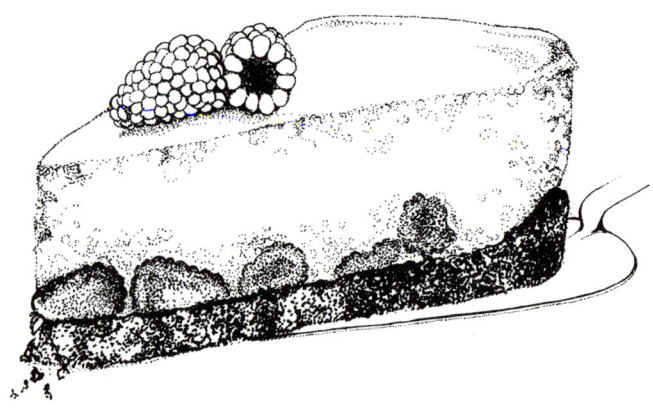

Junket

Ingredients

1pt (0.56l) milk　　　　little nutmeg
1tbs sugar　　　　　　pouring cream
2–3tsp rennet

Method

1 Heat the milk with the sugar until lukewarm or 'blood' heat. Stir in the rennet.
2 Place in a serving dish and sprinkle a little nutmeg on top.
3 Allow to set and serve with the pouring cream.
4 In the West Country junket is served with clotted cream.
Serves 4 portions.

Note Different makes of rennet vary in strength and the cook should refer to the instructions printed on the label. 1tsp of rennet is usually sufficient for 1pt of homogenised, pasteurised or untreated milk. But some rennets require 2–3tsp for the above measures. Junket cannot be made from sterilised or Long Life milk. Rennet can be bought in tablet form which makes it easier for campers to store and carry.

Fried Bananas in Rum

Ingredients

2 large bananas　　　　2tbs rum
1oz (30g) butter　　　　little castor sugar
1tbs lemon juice　　　　cream (optional)

Method

1 Peel and cut the bananas lengthwise.
2 Melt the butter and, when it begins to bubble, fry the bananas for 2 minutes on each side.
3 Add the lemon juice and rum and tilt the pan once the rum is hot in order to ignite.
4 Sprinkle on the castor sugar and serve at once with a little cream if desired.
Serves 2 portions.

Pancakes—Basic Recipe

Ingredients

    4oz (115g) plain flour
    pinch of salt
    1 egg

    ½pt (275ml) milk or milk
     and water
    oil or fat for frying

Method

1 Make the batter by putting the flour and salt in a basin, adding the egg and a little of the milk. Mix to a smooth cream.

2 Add the remaining milk and mix well. Allow to stand a short while before use.

3 In a frying pan melt a little fat or oil and tilt the pan so it covers the base.

4 When fat is really hot pour a little batter into the pan, making sure the mixture spreads evenly.

5 Cook until bubbles rise all over the pancake or until centre looks dry.

6 Toss the pancake over and cook that side. Turn onto a warmed plate and roll.

7 Serve with a sprinkling of castor sugar and a slice of lemon.

Makes 4 to 6 pancakes, depending on size of pan.

5

Salads, Dressed and in the Raw

In the height of summer when most families take out their caravans, salads must appear regularly on the menu. To prevent changing your family into a bunch of rabbits with endless lettuce and tomatoes, try a few variations on the theme. I like to make a complete meal in one salad and serve it on a large platter. There are some very good aluminium ones on the market that can be used and used again, thus saving on the weight of china or heavier metal serving dishes. Platter salads look good and reduce the washing up.

One tip here is if you want crisp lettuce it's much better if you dry it after washing it as then the texture and taste is more pronounced. If you buy a fresh lettuce and want to keep it for a day or two, place it in a saucepan with its lid on and then under the caravan or in a cool place.

Cottage Cheese and Peach Salad

Ingredients

1 lettuce	8 peach halves
1oz (30g) chopped walnuts	1tbs vinegar
1 eating apple, grated or finely chopped	pinch each of mustard, pepper and salt
little lemon juice	1tbs oil
8oz (225g) cottage cheese	2oz (55g) raisins

Method

1 Line a large platter with the lettuce.
2 Mix the chopped walnuts, apple and lemon juice with the cottage cheese and place down the centre of the dish.
3 Place the peach halves, hollow side down, onto the mixture.
4 Put the vinegar, mustard, pepper, salt and oil into a screwtop jar. Shake vigorously and pour over the cheese mixture.
5 Decorate with the raisins.

Serves 4 portions.

Chicken, Orange and Banana Salad

Ingredients

2 cooked chicken portions
¼pt (150ml) mayonnaise
2 large bananas
¼pt (150ml) French dressing

2 oranges
1 lettuce
6oz (170g) cooked long
 grain rice

Method

1 Cut the chicken into bite-size pieces, and mix with the mayonnaise.
2 Peel and chop the bananas and marinade in the French dressing.
3 Peel and chop the oranges.
4 Line a platter with the lettuce, keeping back a few heart leaves.
5 Mix half the orange and banana with the rice and place mixture on the platter.
6 Place the remaining orange and banana on top of the rice, and the chicken mixture on top again.
7 Decorate the whole by putting the lettuce heart on top of the chicken.

Serves 4 portions.

Waldorf Salad

Ingredients

3 large red skinned dessert
 apples
2tbs lemon juice
½ celery head

2oz (55g) chopped walnuts
seasoning
¼pt (150ml) mayonnaise
1 lettuce

Method

1 Slice the apples finely and pour the lemon juice on them.
2 Chop the celery finely and add the walnuts, seasoning and most of the apple.
3 Pour the mayonnaise over the celery mixture and mix well.
4 Line a serving dish with the lettuce leaves and pour the celery mixture in the centre.
5 Overlap the remaining apple slices around the celery mixture.

Serves 4 portions.

Stuffed Pears

Ingredients

2 dessert pears
$\frac{1}{2}$pt (275ml) brine using 1tsp
salt to $\frac{1}{2}$pt (275ml) water
4oz (115g) creamed cheese

1oz (30g) walnuts
a little red pepper or tomato
few lettuce leaves
sprig of parsley

Method

1 Slice the pears lengthwise then peel and put in the brine.
2 Mix the creamed cheese with the chopped walnuts and finely chopped pepper or tomato.
3 Core the pears and fill the cavity with the cheese mixture.
4 Stand the pears on a bed of lettuce and decorate with a sprig of parsley.

Serves 2 portions.

Ham Royal

Ingredients

2oz (55g) Patna rice
1 bayleaf
1 sachet of saffron powder or
1tsp tumeric
½oz (15g) butter
2oz (55g) finely chopped
apple

2oz (55g) finely chopped
onion
1 level tsp curry powder
2tbs cream or top of milk
5 slices cooked ham
pinch of salt

Method

1 Cook the rice with the saffron or tumeric, a pinch of salt and bayleaf. Rinse and cool.
2 Melt the butter in a saucepan and sauté the apple and onion until transparent.
3 Sprinkle the curry powder over the apple mixture and cook for a minute.
4 Remove mixture from the heat and add the cream or top of milk and rice.
5 Chop 1 slice of the ham and add to the apple mixture.
6 Divide the mixture between the remaining slices of ham, roll and place on a serving dish.
7 Garnish with the olives, tomato and parsley.
Serves 4 portions.

Potato Salad

Ingredients

1lb (455g) cooked cold potato,
new ones if possible or waxy
old potatoes
1tbs chopped onion or chives

¼pt (150ml) salad cream or
homemade dressing
salt and pepper

Method

1 Dice the potato and mix with the finely chopped onion or chives.
2 Add the salad cream or homemade dressing and seasonings and mix well.
Serves 4 portions.

Salad Niçoise

Ingredients

2 hard boiled eggs
8oz (225g) French beans
4 tomatoes
1 small onion
½ green pepper
1 lettuce

¼pt (150ml) French dressing
6oz (170g) tin tuna fish
8 anchovy fillets
6 black olives
seasoning

Method

1 Cook the French beans for 6 minutes after topping and tailing them. Let them cool.
2 Skin the tomatoes and cut into quarters. Peel and skin the onion and slice into very thin rings. Seed the pepper and slice.
3 In a bowl place the lettuce leaves and beans and toss in the French dressing.
4 Drain the tuna fish and chop into chunks and add to the lettuce.
5 Add all the other ingredients to the bowl with the exception of a few tomato slices and the eggs.
6 Decorate the whole with the tomato slices and the egg quarters
Serves 4 portions.

Tomato Salad

Ingredients

1lb (455g) finely sliced tomatoes
1 finely chopped onion

½tsp sugar
seasoning
¼pt (150ml) French dressing

Method

1 Place the tomatoes in a bowl and add the onion. Sprinkle on the sugar and seasoning. Pour over the French dressing and mix well.
Serves 3 to 4 portions.

Mushroom Salad

Ingredients

8oz (225g) raw washed
  mushrooms
¼pt (150ml) French dressing

seasoning
pinch of fresh herbs finely
  chopped

Method

1 Place the mushrooms in a bowl. Pour on the French dressing
  and mix well with the seasoning.
2 Sprinkle the chopped herbs on top.
Serves 2 portions.

Mayonnaise

Ingredients

2 egg yolks
½tsp made mustard
¼tsp salt
pinch of pepper

pinch of sugar
¼pt (150ml) olive oil or
  good vegetable oil
2tbs vinegar

Method

1 Place the yolks, seasoning and sugar into a bowl and mix well
  with a whisk or wooden spoon.
2 Add the oil drop by drop, beating very well between each
  addition.
3 Add the vinegar a little at a time and taste.
NB If you like a creamy mayonnaise add a tablespoon of hot
water after the vinegar, but mix it in well.
Dressing for 4 portions.

Aioli Dressing

Ingredients
The same as for Mayonnaise (above) but with the addition of
2 cloves of garlic.

Method
1 Same as for mayonnaise but don't add the hot water.
2 Crush and pound the garlic well and add to the mayonnaise.
NB   Aioli dressing is excellent if used as a dip with fresh vegetables such as small florets of cauliflower, thin strips of carrot, etc.
Dressing for 4 portions.

French Dressing

Ingredients

2tbs olive oil or good vegetable oil	½tsp mustard seasoning
2tbs vinegar	pinch of sugar (optional)

Method
1 Mix all the ingredients together. This is easy if one uses a screwtop jar, otherwise mix well in a small bowl.

Mrs Hallett's Vinaigrette Dressing

Mrs Mary Hallett is my maternal great grandmother

Ingredients

1 whisked egg	2tbs spiced vinegar
¼tsp salt	sugar to taste
1tsp made mustard	cream may be added if available
2tbs olive oil	

Method
1 Place all ingredients together and mix well.
NB   This is best done in a screwtop jar.
Serves 1 portion.

6

My Hissing Friend the
Pressure Cooker

I once heard of a lad who travelled across Europe carrying all his needs on his back, and the piece of equipment he treasured most was his pressure cooker. I know exactly how he felt. With the aid of my hissing friend I am able to cut down my cooking time by half; this gives me more time to lie on the beach allowing the sun to turn me from a recognisable human being into a lobster. I know it is a bulky piece of equipment and also heavy, but the disadvantages are easily outweighed by the advantages. Not only does it cut down on cooking time, it also saves fuel and is able to cook the cheaper, tougher cuts of meat with successful results. Most pressure cookers have small sections that fit inside the saucepan and this enables one to cook a variety of items simultaneously. By cooking vegetables in these sections, one also saves on washing up, which is well worth thinking about when one has to fetch every drop of water required!

I know a lot of cooks are afraid of pressure cookers as they 'blow up'. I have had students who have housed one unused for years until I have insisted they bring it to the college so that I can point out the correct way to use it. They then find it's not such a monster after all and, without exception, have had enough confidence to use it at home.

Make sure your pressure cooker is in good working order. They all have a safety plug—a little rubber washer fixed into the lid with a pin through it. Make sure the pin is set into the rubber and that the rubber is not perished. If you are not sure, buy a new plug; they only cost a few pence. When the pot is boiling this little metal centre will pop up, but don't worry as it will go back into position when the pressure has been released. The next item worth checking is the rubber sealing ring between the pan and the lid. This is also to see that it isn't perished and, when cooking under pressure, doesn't allow the steam to escape. If in doubt renew it. You will need some weights, though some cookers have a press-down flap depending on the make. Finally make sure the hole for the air to escape through is free, and clean it frequently with a pipe cleaner.

One of the problems when using a pressure cooker is the vast amount of steam and condensation it causes, so open windows before commencing. Having done this and checked all the equipment you are ready to start cooking.

GENERAL HINTS

All recipes must use some water and the minimum that can be used in a pressure cooker is ¼pt (150ml). The maximum cooking time is then 10 minutes.

1 See whether you need the trivet in the saucepan.
2 Consult the recipe as to the ingredients needed and the length of cooking time.

Do not fill the pan to more than two-thirds of its capacity with liquid or gravy.

3 Place the ingredients in the saucepan, replace the lid securely and place on the heat, allowing it to come to the boil.
4 When there is a constant flow of steam from the vent, place the required weights on or turn down the key so as to build up the pressure.

At this stage lower the heat.

5 When cooking has been completed remove the saucepan carefully from the heat and reduce the pressure by leaving it to cool for a few minutes. I prefer to run cold water over the side of the pan as this rapidly decreases the pressure to normal. The pan itself can also be placed into cold water, but do not pour water over the weights. On a site it's advisable to have the water ready at hand.

Most recipes can be used with a pressure cooker by cutting the cooking time by half. Here are a few tips worth noting.

1 Sauté and fry vegetables and meat well before adding the liquid since during cooking they don't brown.
2 Add all thickening towards the end of the cooking time and then reheat without the lid. I find this prevents the food from sticking to the base of the pan.
3 Add salt to the food and not to the water, as the water doesn't penetrate into the food as with ordinary cooking.

57

All times given are from the time the cooking is under pressure.

Soups

Stock (2 hours)
Place the marrow bones in the pressure cooker and cover with cold water. When cooked remove the bones and allow the liquid to set. Skim off the fat and use when required. If keeping for a few days, bring to the boil and simmer a few minutes before use.

Carrot (6 minutes)
8oz (225g) grated or finely cut carrot
1 onion, finely chopped, or 2 leeks
2½pt (1.4l) stock
3 level tbs uncooked Patna rice
1 bayleaf
seasoning

Tomato (5 minutes)
2lb (1kg) tomatoes
1½pt (0.9l) water or chicken stock
1 finely chopped rasher of bacon
1 level tbs sago
pinch of herbs (preferably basil or thyme)
2tsps sugar
seasoning

Minestrone (20 minutes)
2lb (1kg) finely chopped mixed vegetables
8oz (225g) finely sliced shin of beef
2pt (1.1l) water or stock
8oz (225g) broken spaghetti or small pasta
seasoning

Scotch broth (20 minutes)
1lb (455g) scrag end of mutton
1 large onion, finely chopped
1 small chopped turnip
1 large carrot, sliced
2tbs pearl barley
2½pt (1.4l) water or chicken stock
seasoning

Vegetable (15 minutes)
2 onions, finely sliced
2 or 3 carrots, finely chopped
1 or 2 tomatoes
1lb (455g) potatoes
1 finely chopped turnip, swede or parsnip, or collection of all three
2pt (1.1l) water or stock
seasoning

Fish

All recipes use one-third of a pint (200ml) of water which later can be used in a sauce.

Fillets of plaice (3 minutes). Roll from the tail end, place on a trivet. If necessary separate the fillets with greaseproof paper. Serve with a sauce.

Steaks of cod, turbot, halibut, haddock etc (4 minutes). Place on greased trivet.

Smoked haddock (5 minutes). Place some butter on the fish and cook in a mixture of a $\frac{1}{4}$pt (150ml) of water and milk mixed without using the trivet.

Salmon steaks (8 minutes). Place on a trivet and sprinkle with lemon.

Fish steaks and vegetables (4 minutes). Use the trivet. Place the fish on it and surround with the finely chopped vegetables.

Poultry

Recipes use $\frac{1}{2}$pt (275ml) of water.

Boiling fowl (8 to 10 minutes per lb, 455g). Rub the breast with butter and place on a trivet. Drain well. Can be browned in an oven.

Chicken portion (5 minutes). Place on the trivet. If very young wrap in tinfoil or greased paper.

Pigeon, pheasant or other game (5 minutes). Use the trivet. Ideal way to tenderise an old bird before roasting.

Vegetables

All recipes use ½pt (275ml) of water, and no trivet unless stated.

	Minutes		Minutes
Artichokes, globe	7–10	Kohl-rabi	5
Artichokes, Jerusalem	4–6	Leeks, whole	6
Beetroot	15	Onions	5
Broad beans	4	Parsnips	4–5
Carrots	4	Patotoes, halved	6
Cauliflower, quartered	4	Potatoes, new	5–6
Cauliflower, whole	5–6	Pumpkin, cubed	4
Corn on the cob	8	Root vegetables,	
French or runner beans	4	parsnips, swedes,	
Green vegetables,		turnips, cubed	5–4
broccoli, Brussels		Spinach	1
sprouts, cabbage, etc.	4	Vegetable marrow, cubed	4

Pulses and Cereals

Dried pulses and vegetables. Allow 2pt (1l) of water to each 8oz (225g). Place in the pressure cooker and allow to soak for 30 to 45 minutes. Then bring to the boil and cook.

	Minutes
Butter beans, haricot beans, peas	20
Split peas, lentils	15

Cereals. Allow 2pt (1l) of water to 8oz (225g) cereal. Bring the water to the boil and cook.

	Minutes
Macaroni, spaghetti, vermicelli etc	10
Pearl barley etc	20
Rice, allow 1½pt (0.8l) water to 8oz (225g):	
Long grain	3
Pudding rice	4
Natural brown rice	5

Meat Dishes

Beef stew (no trivet is needed). Use stewing steak, selection of vegetables, stock, seasoning.

Toss meat in seasoned flour. Brown the meat and onion in hot fat. Remove pan from heat, add stock, seasoning and other vegetables. Cook for 20 minutes. Thicken after cooking if necessary.

Rabbit stew. Use jointed rabbit, vegetables, stock, seasoning. Method the same as beef stew, cook for 20 minutes.

Steak and kidney pudding using a suet crust and raw meat. Cook for 15 minutes without the pressure and 45 minutes under pressure. Put 1½pt (0.8l) of water in the pan and use the trivet.

Pot roasts (topside, brisket, etc). Brown the meat in hot fat. Remove pan from the heat. Place trivet in pot, pour in 1pt (0.5l) water, replace the meat and cook for 12 minutes per lb. (If the meat is fatty, remove fat before adding the water.) Cook mutton the same way, but allow 10 minutes per lb.

Salt-beef and dumplings. Use silverside, carrots, turnips, onions, etc and dumplings. Remove trivet. Cover meat with cold water, bring to the boil then throw the water away. Cover with new water, add the vegetables and cook for 15 minutes per lb. Add the dumplings after the pressure has been reduced and cook for 20 minutes in an open cooker.

Minced meat. Minced fresh beef, small cubes of vegetables, ½pt (275ml) stock, seasoning. Brown the mince in hot fat; strain off excessive fat. Take off the heat and add the vegetables and stock. Cook for 7 minutes. Thicken with flour if necessary.

Chops, liver and steak. Remove trivet. Toss the meat in seasoned flour and fry in hot fat in an open cooker. Remove meat and fry the vegetables. Lay the trivet on top of the vegetables and meat on top. Add a little liquid and cook under pressure for 7 minutes.

Oxtail (vegetables optional). Without the trivet place the oxtail in the cooker and cover with water. Cook for 40 minutes. It is best to allow it to cool, and remove the surplus fat and reheat the next day.

Sweets and Puddings

Steamed puddings. Place mixture in pudding basin and stand on trivet. Use ¼pt (150ml) of water for every 15 minutes cooking time plus ½pt (275ml). Steam without pressure for 15 minutes then for 25 minutes under pressure.

Suet pudding. Same method as above but 15 minutes steaming and 35 minutes under pressure.

Egg custard. Same method as above but only cook for 5 minutes under pressure. No steaming time.

7
Barbecues Without Smoke and Burnt Offerings

I often wonder why more campers and caravanners do not have barbecues. Of course you need the correct equipment as there could be a great fire risk, and a lot of sites forbid them completely. I remember a site near St Léonard D'Norbat where a Frenchman in the caravan opposite me got out all his barbecue equipment and prepared to cook his evening meal. With bits of wood he got his charcoal glowing and when it was a bright amber he popped into his caravan and came out with a chicken in one hand and a large glass of wine in the other. He placed the chicken over the coals and settled himself down with a drink and a book as he guarded his supper. He must have realised that the smells from that chicken that drifted over to us were most appetising and even to this day a chicken has never smelt so good. Each time he turned the spit I had a desire to rush over and bite a chunk off his supper. The whole business, although it took time, seemed so worthwhile.

I have a gas poker that has been adapted to go on my gas cylinder. By using it one saves work searching for wood and setting light to the charcoal base as I can put the poker amongst the fuel and light it that way. A barbecue on a beach is well worthwhile, as often there is driftwood and other litter that will make a base to a fire. You may build one with pebbles but beware of the fact that some stones are apt to explode when they get very hot. You can make a very simple barbecue by building two small pillars of bricks and suspending a wiremesh tray between them. Make sure the whole outfit is stable before you commence cooking. Other equipment that is a 'must' is an old squeezy bottle full of water to extinguish the flames that catch the food we are cooking, then we get that super barbecue flavour without burnt offerings.

Meat Balls with a Sweet Sour Sauce

Ingredients

Meat balls:
2tbs oil
1 small onion, finely chopped
8oz (225g) finely minced
  steak or good minced meat
1 egg
pinch of nutmeg
seasoning
little flour for dusting

Sauce:
1tbs sugar
2tbs vinegar
1tbs cornflour
1tbs soy sauce
$\frac{1}{4}$pt (150ml) water
1tbs tomato purée

Method

1 Fry the onion until brown in 1tbs of the oil.
2 Mix all the meat ball ingredients together and shape into rounds, dusting them in a little flour.
3 Melt the remaining oil and fry the meat balls until crisp. Drain and keep warm.
4 Mix all the sauce ingredients together, bring to the boil and allow to thicken.
5 Place the balls on a serving plate and pour the sauce over. Serve with rice or pasta.

When we cook these at home on our barbecue we have a small sheet of metal and cook all meat balls and burgers on it.

Serves 4 portions.

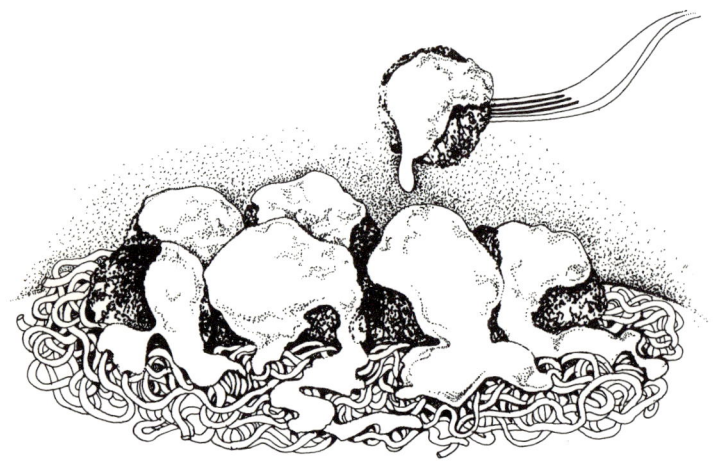

Lamb Chops and Whole Onions

Ingredients

2 lamb chops per person   2 small Spanish onions,
                                         with skins on, per person

Method

1 Choose chops that have been thinly sliced, eg meaty chump, loin and cutlets. Trim off any excess fat as they will only catch fire when the fat melts.
2 Make sure the fire is ready for cooking, no smoke and only embers glowing. Even if it looks past cooking, the fat and juices will liven up the dullest fire.
3 Oil the meat and place on the grill. Make sure you seal the chops well, then cook, turning them over to cook both sides.
4 Place the onions whole over the fire and don't worry when the skins catch. Allow to cook through, turning frequently.
5 Remove the skins from the onions and serve with the chops.

NB   Chops are much more tasty if marinaded for a few hours before cooking, but on a site this could cause problems so it's better not to bother.

Spareribs

Ingredients

8 to 12 spareribs (pork)   little salt
1 crushed clove garlic   1 tsp dry mustard
1 tsp paprika pepper   1 tbs brown sugar

Method

1 Mix the garlic, pepper, salt, mustard and sugar together and rub into the spareribs.
2 Cook the ribs for 15 minutes, turning frequently and basting with a little oil.

These are delicious if served with a barbecue sauce.

Serves 4 portions.

Barbecue Sauce

Ingredients

1oz (30g) butter
1 large onion, finely chopped
1tbs vinegar
1tbs Worcester sauce
2tbs tomato purée

2tbs lemon juice
1oz (30g) brown sugar
¼pt (150ml) water
little salt

Method

1 Melt the butter in a saucepan and sauté the finely chopped onion until golden.
2 Add the remaining ingredients, bring to the boil and simmer for 15 minutes.

Serves 3 to 4 portions.

Satay Chicken

Ingredients

8oz (225g) lean chicken

little oil

Sauce:
1 onion, finely chopped
2 cloves of crushed garlic
2tbs oil
¼pt (150ml) dry white wine
 or dry cider

2tbs sherry
2tbs soy sauce
2tbs tomato purée
4tbs peanut butter

Method

1 Cut the chicken into ½in (1.2cm) cubes and thread several onto skewers. Brush with a little oil and cook until golden.
2 Sauté the onion and garlic in a saucepan, with the oil, until golden. Add the wine or cider, sherry, soy sauce and tomato purée, bring to the boil and reduce by a third. Mix in the peanut butter and stir well until smooth. It is then ready for use.

Serves 4 portions.

Kebabs with Savoury Rice

Ingredients

8oz (225g) lean lamb
1 kidney
2 rashers bacon
4 small onions
2 firm tomatoes

1 green pepper
4oz (115g) button mushrooms
1tbs oil
1 small tin of pineapple
  rings

Savoury rice:
2oz (55g) long grain rice
1oz (30g) butter
1 small finely chopped onion

1oz (30g) mushrooms
1oz (30g) raisins
seasoning

Method

1 Chop the lamb into 1in (2.5cm) cubes. Skin, core and cut the kidney into slices.
2 Seed the pepper and slice half of it.
3 Using four skewers, thread on the lamb, kidneys, bacon rolls, onions, tomatoes, pepper slices, pineapple chunks, and mushrooms in between the meat.
4 Brush with the oil and place over the fire.
5 Cook the rice in a little water with the seasoning; drain and allow to dry a little.
6 Melt the butter and sauté the chopped onion until golden, then add the chopped mushrooms, remaining green pepper, chopped, and raisins. Add the rice and cook for a few minutes. Place the rice mixture on a serving dish and lay the kebabs across it.

This dish is delicious if served with a little barbecue sauce.
Serves 4 portions.

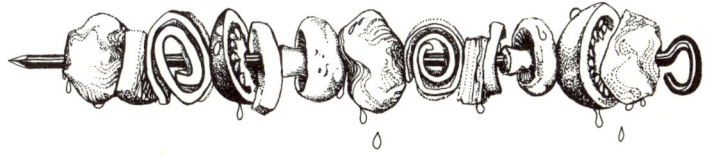

Dampers

Ingredients

1lb (455g) plain flour,
  preferably strong flour
pinch of salt
1tsp bicarbonate of soda

3oz (85g) butter, margarine
  or lard
little milk, preferably sour

Method

1 Mix the flour, salt and soda together. Rub in the fat and mix with the milk to a stiff dough.
2 Make into 4 rounds and bake slowly on a low fire, turning occasionally.
Serves 4 portions.

Hot Garlic Bread

Ingredients

1 loaf of French bread
4oz (115g) butter

salt
2 cloves of garlic

Method

1 Cut the bread into 1in (2.5cm) slices, but do not cut through the bottom crust.
2 Cream butter, salt and garlic well together and spread between the slices.
3 Wrap the loaf firmly in two layers of tin foil and allow to cook for 15 to 20 minutes, turning it over once.
4 To serve, remove foil, cut through the slices and serve at once.
Serves 4 to 6 portions.

Bread Twists on Sticks

Ingredients

8oz (225g) self-raising flour   4 clean sticks
little water

Method

1 Mix the flour with the water until a stiff dough. Twist the dough into 4 strips each 6in (15cm) long and wrap around the sticks.
2 Cook the sticks over a low fire, constantly turning. To test they are cooked insert a knife into the dough and, if it comes out clean, they are ready.

Serves 2 portions.

Fruit on Skewers

Ingredients

A selection of fresh fruit such as
bananas, apricots, peaches
and pineapple

little melted butter
little brown sugar

Method

1 Chop the fruit into chunks and place on the skewers. Brush with the melted butter.
2 Place over the fire for a few minutes until soft. Roll in the brown sugar and return to the fire to crystallise the sugar. Serve at once.

They are delicious if served with fresh cream.

Parcel cookery is wrapping the food securely in greased aluminium foil. It's an excellent way of cooking because one can vary the contents, for example chops can be accompanied with sliced vegetables and all the flavour and juices are sealed in. It's a chance to cook chops, sausages, steaks, fish, etc to individual taste—if someone likes garlic then include it in that parcel but omit it in the others. Small quantities of stock, cream or wine can be added to the meat or fish, and during the cooking they will be absorbed. The French term for this type of cooking is 'en papillote' and here are the main rules for successful results.

1 Use the foil in double thickness.
2 Make sure the edges are securely sealed.
3 Add a little butter or a few drops of liquid to the parcel as it might dry out slightly while cooking, even if the edges are firmly closed.
4 Cook over a low even heat and turn frequently.
5 The cooking time will vary with the contents, but 30 minutes is a good guide.

Baked Trout with Almonds

Ingredients

1 trout per person	1oz (30g) butter
few fresh herbs (optional)	1oz (30g) almonds, flaked
seasoning	are best

Method

1 Clean the fish well but leave whole. Place the herbs and seasoning in the belly of the fish, though this is not necessary as they mar the subtle flavour.
2 Lay the trout on a double layer of foil, spreading both sides with the butter, season and sprinkle the almonds on top. Secure well and place over a slow fire.
3 Cook for 40 minutes approximately, turning once.

Baked Potatoes

Ingredients

   1 potato per person   seasoning
   1tbs oil

Method

1 Scrub the potato well and dry. Prick well with a fork; this will prevent it from bursting while cooking.
2 Place the potato on a double layer of foil, rub the oil well into it and season well. Wrap securely in the foil.
3 Cook over a low heat or in the embers for 45 minutes approximately, depending on size. When cooked remove the foil and serve with:
Melted butter and seasonings
Sour cream mixed with chives
Chopped parsley and seasonings
Grated cheese
Crispy bacon
If one cares to scoop out the pulp, the potato can be refilled with fillings as above and scrambled egg, sliced cooked mushrooms, cottage cheese, sliced tomatoes, etc.

8

Existing on One Burner

It's not impossible to serve a very elaborate meal using only one burner, but it needs a good deal of planning and thought beforehand. Most of the recipes in this book can be used providing the camper has two pans. Take a curry for example. Cook the curry first until it's nearly completed, then take it off the heat and place a lid on it, keeping it away from draughts. Now cook the rice and, while draining it, reheat the curry. Remember to cook the dish that needs the most cooking first.

When frying, especially eggs, bacon and fried bread, sort out the order before you start. Commence with the bacon and, when cooked on both sides, place the bread and egg in the pan and rest the bacon on top of the bread where it will keep warm. Remove the bacon for a few minutes while you cook the other side and then put it back on top of the bread. Likewise chops and sauté potatoes, or even chips if thinly sliced, can be cooked in one pan.

All stews are ideal for one burner, and don't forget potatoes can be cooked with the stew. Dumplings are excellent, since they can be added towards the end of the stewing time. Small pieces of pasta can be cooked in a stew. If cooking a rice dish, try the risottos, since then all the meal is cooked in one pot. Soups need not be watery. Make a good substantial one that can be eaten with large chunks of bread.

Often one hasn't room but, if this is not a problem, a pressure cooker or heavy large frying pan can be an asset if using only one heat source.

I've existed quite happily on a site with only one burner and find the cooking more interesting because it certainly presents a challenge.

Dumplings

Ingredients

4oz (115g) self-raising flour
or 4oz (115g) plain flour
and ¾tsp baking powder
2oz (55g) suet

¼tsp salt
pinch of pepper
water to mix

Method

1 Stir all dry ingredients together and mix to a stiff dough with the water.
2 Divide the mixture into 8 to 12 dumplings and drop into the bubbling stew.
3 Cook for 20 minutes, keeping the lid on the saucepan and the stew boiling.

Serves 4 portions.

Hunters' Stew

Ingredients

¾lb (340g) stewing beef
  (chuck, skirt, leg, etc)
1oz (30g) flour
1 medium onion
2tbs oil
1 swede or turnip

1 large carrot
½tsp salt
¼tsp pepper
¾pt (425ml) beef stock

Method

1 Chop the onion and brown in the hot oil. Toss the cubed meat in the flour, add to the onion and cook until evenly brown.
2 Cube the vegetables and add these and the seasonings to the pan.
3 Pour in the stock, stirring well, and bring to the boil. Let it simmer for 1½ to 2 hours depending on the cut of meat. This process can be hurried up if the meat is cut into smaller cubes.

Serves 3 to 4 portions.

Irish Stew

Ingredients
- 1lb (455g) scrag or middle neck of lamb or mutton
- 8oz (225g) onions
- 1lb (455g) potatoes
- salt and pepper
- 1pt (575ml) beef stock

Method
1 Cut the meat into cubes, slice the onions into rings and halve the potatoes.
2 Put the meat and vegetables in alternate layers in the pan, season well and pour the stock over it.
3 Bring the pot to the boil with the lid on, then turn down the heat and simmer for 1 hour.
4 Do not stir during the cooking time, but if worried that the stew may stick shake the pan occasionally.

Serves 4 portions.

Lamb Ratatouille

Ingredients
- 4 lamb cutlets
- 1 green pepper
- 1lb (455g) onions
- 4 courgettes
- 1 clove of garlic
- 1lb (455g) tomatoes
- 1tbs oil
- seasoning

Method
1 Prepare the vegetables—slice and seed the green pepper, slice the onions and tomatoes. Do not peel the courgettes, just slice them. Peel and crush the garlic.
2 Heat the oil in the pan and fry the cutlets well on both sides, remove and keep warm.
3 Fry the onions and garlic in the oil and, when transparent, add the rest of the vegetables and seasoning. Place the lid on the pan and allow the vegetables to sweat for 10 minutes.
4 Replace the cutlets, cover the pan with a lid and continue to cook for another 20 minutes.

Serves 4 portions.

Goulash

Ingredients

1lb (455g) lean stewing meat, beef or veal or a mixture of both
2tbs flour
1lb (455g) onions
2tbs oil
1tsp salt
1½tsp paprika pepper

1½pt (0.85l) stock
¼pt (150ml) of red wine or tomato juice or mixture of both
1lb (455g) fresh tomatoes or small tin of tomatoes
1 clove of garlic
a little cream (optional)

Method

1 Cut the meat into 1in (2.5cm) cubes. Slice the onion and fry in the oil until light brown.
2 Add the meat and cook until evenly browned, then add the flour, salt and paprika.
3 Add the stock and wine or tomato juice; bring to the boil.
4 Slice the tomatoes and add the garlic, which is best crushed.
5 Bring the pan to the boil and cook for 1 hour or until meat is tender.

This dish is improved if you add a few tablespoonfuls of cream before serving.

Serves 4 portions.

Tipsy Pork Chops

Ingredients

4 loin or chump pork chops
2tbs oil
1tsp made mustard
1 sliced onion

1tbs flour
pinch of herbs
$\frac{1}{2}$pt (275ml) cider
2 cooking apples

Method

1 Melt 1 tablespoon of the oil and fry the chops on both sides until well done. Remove and keep warm, having spread them with the mustard.
2 Add the rest of the oil and fry the onion. When transparent add the flour and cook for a couple of minutes.
3 Add the herbs and cider and cook until the sauce thickens. Add the finely sliced apples and allow them to poach in the sauce.
4 Return the chops to the pan and simmer for 10 to 15 minutes. It may be necessary to add more cider or water to the sauce.

Serves 4 portions.

Country Soup

Ingredients

1tbs butter
1tbs oil
1 small swede
2 potatoes
1 small turnip
1 large onion

2 large carrots
1$\frac{1}{2}$ to 2pt (0.85–1l) stock
  (chicken)
1tbs tomato purée
salt and pepper
pinch of herbs

Method

1 Melt the fats together and sauté the finely chopped vegetables until they are soft. Then add the rest of the ingredients and cook for 15 to 20 minutes.
2 Mash down half the soup so that it is a thick consistency. If necessary thicken with a little cornflour.

NB The recipe can be made by sautéing the vegetables and adding a packet of instant soup.

Serves 4 portions.

9

Fish and the Best Way To Cook Them

We are fortunate to live on an island and have a vast variety of sea fish surrounding us. There are also many freshwater fish in our rivers and lakes, etc, which are referred to as coarse fish. The season for these is from mid-June to mid-March and you will need a licence to catch them. On the whole fish caught with rod, line and bait have a muddy taste and need to be well washed before eating. Those caught with rod, line and fly are referred to as game fish and are usually free from that taste and have a very delicate delicious flavour. If you wish to catch game fish you will need a licence and permission to fish in a particular stretch of water. Enquire the price before you commit yourself, since it can be an expensive sport. The season varies from place to place, but the close season is usually between November and January.

If you are not lucky enough to catch your own, be careful when buying. Fresh fish should be firm to the touch with full shiny eyes and bright red gills. There are various cuts of fish just as there are of meat. Fillets are slices from the fish but without bones; they vary in size and thickness according to the type of fish. Steaks are cut from a round fish and are taken from between the middle part of the body and the tail. Cutlets are taken from between the middle part of the body and the head. Many fish can be served whole or with just the head removed.

I have divided the sea fish into two sections for easier identification. On the whole most oily fish and white fish come from the sea, but there are exceptions. Many fish are available throughout the year. They are, on the whole, at their best and most plentiful at the seasons I have given.

SEA FISH

Oily Varieties

Conger eel
This fish varies considerably in size and, with its snake-like body, resembles the land eel. It is brown or sometimes purple or grey on its back and white on its belly. The flesh is rather tough and is better stewed or baked. If using steaks, cut them into ½in (1cm) thickness and fry or grill slowly over a low heat. Season: March to October.

Gurnard
There are several varieties of gurnard. The grey gurnard is grey or dark brown in colour. The tub gurnard is yellowish and has beautifully striped fins. The most common is the red gurnard, which is a bright-red colour. It has a very tough skin and the spines on its back make it difficult to handle. The flesh is sweet-tasting. Season in the south is between July and November.

Herring
The back of the herring is blue or greenish-blue and the sides and belly are silver. It usually weighs between 6 and 8oz. One of our commonest fish but, due to extensive fishing, supplies are not so plentiful. Herring are mostly served whole and can be fried, baked or grilled. Season: April to October.

There are various kinds of preserved herrings known under other names:

Bismarck herring   Flat herrings marinated in spiced vinegar and onion rings.

Bloaters   Herrings salted and slightly smoked.

Kippers   Herrings that have been salted and smoked longer than a bloater and therefore keep longer. They can be bought filleted.

Red herring   Herrings dried, smoked whole, and dyed red. They are mostly used as starters or in patés.

Rollmop   Herrings that are kept whole but boned and then rolled. They are preserved in spiced vinegar and chopped onions.

Salt herrings   Herrings kept whole and soaked in a good brine. They need to be well soaked before use.

Mackerel

Very common fish, usually caught in shoals. They have a long slinky body in a greenish-blue colour with a dark-blue wavy line along their backs. They can be fried, grilled or baked as a whole or without the head; delicious if baked in spiced vinegar and allowed to cool and then eaten cold. Best eaten the day they are caught. Season: April to July.

Smoked mackerel These are whole mackerel that have been soaked in brine and then smoked. They are eaten cold with a salad or made into paté.

Mullet (red)

A bright-red fish with the scales on its back edged in brown. In shape similar to a herring, but it has a very blunt snout. It has white, well-flavoured flesh. The best way to cook mullet is to bake or grill it. Season: October to December.

Pilchards

These fish can be found off the West Country's coast but they are mostly canned and not sold fresh. Their backs are greenish and their sides silvery. They grow to 14in (36cm) but are usually caught at 8in (20cm). They appear in shoals during the summer in the English Channel and, if available fresh, can be grilled or lightly fried.

Smelts

Small herring-type fish with a greenish or grey-green back, silvery sides and a white belly. Deliciously flavoured with white flesh. Sometimes they are called sparling. Season: January to March.

Sprats

Usually between 4 and 5in (10–13cm) in length. They are blue or greenish-blue on the back and silver on the sides and belly. They are served whole, having first been tossed in seasoned flour and then fried. Season: November to March.

White Fish (non-oily)

Bass (sea wolf, sea perch and white salmon)
A fish frequently caught off our coasts. Silver in colour with 8 to 9 spines on its back. At its smallest is 10in (25cm) from nose to tip of tail but can grow to weigh 18lb (8kg). The flesh is pink and very delicate in flavour. Bass can be cooked whole or cut into steaks and cutlets. Either grill, fry, poach or bake. Season: May to August.

Bream (pandora, dorade and chad)
A very bony fish but with a delicate pink flesh. Not held in much esteem. It can be grilled, fried, baked or stuffed. Season: June to December.

Brill
This fish resembles a turbot but is much rounder in shape. It's greyish-yellow in colour with light spots and speckles; the underside is opaque white. Served whole either grilled, fried, baked or stuffed. Season: October to May.

Catfish (rockfish)
A bluish-grey fish with black transverse stripes over its body and fins. Colour is very reminiscent of a tabby cat. Another variety is the spotted catfish which has dark-brown spots rather than stripes. The flesh is pinkish and is best used in stews and soups. Season: September to February.

Cod
A visitor to our coasts from early November to early spring, and recognisable by its greenish or reddish mottled upper parts and a white line that runs down its side. It is a large fish that can weigh up to 88lb (40kg). Cod is usually sold by the piece, either as steaks, cutlets or fillets. It can be poached, baked, grilled or fried. Is available throughout the year, but its season is from October to January.

Coley
Round in shape, with a grey skin. The flesh is a greyish colour but goes whiter when cooked. It is one of the cheapest fish on the

market and is excellent in fishcakes and pies. Can be fried, poached and baked. Is ideal if dipped in batter and deep fried.

Dabs

Flat-fish that look like small plaice but have a sweeter taste. They are often confused with small plaice and flounders, but can easily be distinguished by rubbing a finger from head to tail, as the scales on the back have backward-pointing teeth and feel very rough. The back is light brown with dark-brown spots, but sometimes these spots are yellow or orange. Dabs can be cooked in various ways, but lightly floured and then grilled or fried is one of the best ways of serving them. They can be filleted or left whole. Season: June to February.

Dogfish (flake, rock eel, huss)

There are two varieties of dogfish. The lesser spotted dogfish has many small dark-brown spots on a lighter brown background with a pale belly. The black-mouthed dogfish has a pattern of dark-brown blotches with lighter borders. The inside of the mouth is black. Flesh is white and usually sold on the bone. It has a creamy flesh and the fish is best served fried or baked. Season: July to November.

Flounder (fluke)

A flat-fish belonging to the same family as the brill and plaice. Body is usually brownish olive-green with a few pale-orange spots. The underside is a more opaque white than that of the plaice, and it hasn't such a good flavour. Can be dusted with flour and fried or grilled. Season: March to April.

Garfish

A long slender fish with a very pointed jaw, resembling a sand eel. The upper part is bright blue-green and the sides silver. It is very good to eat but, when cooked, the bones are turquoise green. It is best cooked as steaks and fried, grilled or baked. Season: July to November.

John Dory

A most odd-looking fish. The body is as deep as it is long but extremely narrow as if made from cardboard. It has a large head and mouth. Is greyish or olive-brown with a yellow metallic sheen. There are two spots behind the head; these are black with a yellow halo around them. Legend says that St Peter caught the dory from the Sea of Galilee and left his thumb-marks. However it is doubtful if this fish has ever been in the Sea of Galilee. It is good to eat and tastes like plaice but, due to its thick body, needs a long slow grilling; or it can be filleted. Season: July to November.

Haddock
Has a brownish-olive back, silvery sides and belly. It also has a black lateral line running from the top of the gill to the centre of the tail. Behind the gill on either side of the head is a black spot. Legend has it that these too were thumb-prints made by St Peter when he picked the haddock out of the sea. It can be bread-crumbed and baked with or without forcemeat, fried or even boiled. In season from June to February. Haddock is delicious when cured and Finnan Haddock and Arbroath Smokies are well-known throughout the world.

Hake
A long slender fish. The body is slate blue or grey with silvery sides and belly. It has a thin black lateral line from head to tail. The flesh has an excellent flavour and very few bones. Grows to over 1yd (1m) long and is therefore sold as steaks and cutlets. Season: July to March.

Halibut
A large flat-fish that weighs approximately 9lb (4kg) but can grow to 400lb (181kg). It has an olive-green upper side and white underside. The flesh is white and should be firm. Is served whole, having first been poached, or as steaks. Season: August to April.

Ling
Looks like a hake but grows much larger, even as long as 6ft (2m). Its long slender body has a grey, brown or bronze-green upper part with dark marbled patterns. Ling are very good eaten as steaks or cutlets and are often salted. Season: July to November.

Monk fish

This huge ugly fish is a cross between a dogfish and a flat-fish. The head is very large and broad but the tail is thin and small. The skin is very tough. The upper sides are grey and the belly is white. Best fried or baked as steaks. Season: July to November.

Plaice

The best known of the flat-fish. The upper side is an olive greenish-brown with bright-red or orange spots. The belly is a dull creamy white. Is cooked whole or filleted, and at its best fried, grilled or in batter. Season: January to April.

Pollack (lythe)

Looks very similar to a whiting. Is muddy brown or muddy green in colour. It's not sold commercially but is a favourite with anglers. Pollack can grow to a large size and are best filleted then fried or grilled. Season: July to November.

Skate

This fish is slate blue or grey with grey and black spots; belly is slate grey. The skin is smooth but has patches of prickles. It is kite-shaped and grows to a huge size. Flesh is pink but only the wings are eaten. It can be fried, poached or grilled. Season: October to April.

Sole

A common flat-fish, olive-brown with black markings on the upper side, and with a white belly. Is known as a dover sole or black sole. The skin is slimy and difficult to remove. Serve whole or as fillets. It has a very delicate flavour so it's best to grill it in butter. Season: July to March.

Lemon sole   Is wider than the dover sole, and light brown with dark-brown spots on the upper sides. It has not as much flavour as the dover sole. Season: December to March.

Witch sole   Similar to lemon sole but thinner. Not as good in flavour as the other soles. Season: August to April.

Turbot

A most sought-after fish because of its excellent flavour. A large diamond-shaped fish with light-brown speckly skin on the upper side and a creamy-white belly. It is served whole or as fillets or steaks. Can be poached, baked or grilled. Season: April to July.

Whiting

A round fish belonging to the cod family. The upper parts are a golden olive-green and the sides and belly silver with a gold sheen. Has a very delicate flavour when first caught but soon loses it. Rather bony but can be filleted. It is best to poach, bake or fry this fish. Season: all the year round.

COARSE FISH

Bream

There are two kinds of bream: one is almost brown and the other silver or white. They are good to eat if well washed and can be stuffed, baked or boiled and served with a sauce.

Carp

Usually found in ponds and lakes. The body is smooth and generally whitish in colour. Owing to their habit of burying themselves in mud they often taste muddy and the gills must be skilfully removed as this is the muddiest part. The head is considered the best part of the fish. They can be baked with or without forcemeat, fried, grilled or boiled. Related to the carp is the barbel, but it has a more streamlined body, with deep bronzy-olive back, golden sides and white belly.

Chub

Has a deep olive-green back, and yellow sides changing to silver and white. The belly fins are pink while the other fins are deep-green, almost black. It is best boiled and served with a sauce.

Dace (dart, dare)

A silver, slender-built fish. Not worth cooking but, if you are desperate, fry or boil it.

Eel

A mysterious fish. It breeds in the Sargasso Sea and its young, the elvers, reach this country in the spring. They remain in our rivers and ponds until they get the urge to spawn and they then make their way back to the Sargasso. While at sea they are slate-blue, but once in our ponds and rivers they are an olive-brownish colour. They are an oily fish and well worth eating. Remove the skin and either boil, bake or fry them or use as a pie filling.

Elvers   Scald them, then scramble them with egg, pepper and salt.

Grayling
Varies in colour depending on its surroundings, but is mostly grey, though it can be olive gold to purple. It tastes similar to trout and is in season when trout is not. May be baked, boiled or fried.

Perch
This is the best coarse fish for eating. It has good flavoured, white, firm flesh and tastes similar to turbot. Has an olive-green back, bronze and yellow sides, white belly and orange fins. It can be boiled, baked, fried or stewed.

Pike
Tastes similar to mackerel. It is green and brown in colour with a long narrow body and head; it has a snapping jaw and razor-like teeth. Can be baked or boiled.

Roach
A silver fish with a bluish-green back and white belly. It also has red lower fins. In deep water it becomes darker. Often mistaken for rudd but the fin on a roach's back is directly above the lower front fin. The flesh is white but turns red when boiled. Is best boiled or fried.

Tench
Smaller than a carp but tastes very muddy. It changes colour to suit its surroundings but at its best has a greenish-bronze body, pale underside and orange-red fins. It can change to a deep olive-black. Best to clean it well and then boil and serve with a sauce.

As you can see, most coarse fish, with the exception of a few, aren't worth cooking. My husband, who is a keen fisherman, says, 'Boil any coarse fish with a piece of plywood, then throw away the fish and eat the board.' I'm apt to agree, but how can you tell young Johnny, when he shows you his first catch and asks if you will cook it for supper, that it's not worthwhile? At least you now know how to cook it.

Game fish are the complete opposite, with their delicious delicate flavour.

GAME FISH

Salmon

The salmon is a migratory fish which spawns and spends its early life in fresh water, then leaves its river and goes miles into the deep ocean. There it grows quickly on a rich diet of shrimps and small fish. After a time in the ocean the urge to spawn drives it back up the river of its birth to spawn and re-start the cycle of life. A curious feature of the salmon's life cycle is that, having left the sea to spawn, it doesn't eat again until it returns; because of this the best salmon to eat is one caught in estuaries or rivers, having recently left the sea. (The distinct North Pacific salmon group never returns to the sea but dies after spawning.)

During its strange life cycle the salmon has many names. After it has hatched and until it is ready to go to sea it is called a 'parr'. At this stage it is very like a brown trout except that it has larger spots or blotches down its side. By the time it is ready for its journey to the ocean it has changed to a silvery blue and is called a 'smolt'. When it returns to the river for the first time it is a handsome blue-backed fish with red or brown spots and silvery belly, weighing 4 to 8lb (2–4kg) and called a 'grilse'.

A true salmon is one which, having spent more time in the sea, has grown bigger than a grilse and has returned to the river for a second time. During its spawning time in the river the salmon gradually turns red and loses condition. After spawning it is a dull, weak, red fish and unfit for eating.

Salmon is an expensive fish to buy and the male is better than the female. It can be cooked in so many different ways: poached, grilled, baked or even boiled. It needs a sauce served with it. Smoked salmon is also very good and is served as a starter, having been cut into thin slices.

Trout

There are several kinds of trout. The brown trout, which is common in still and running water, has a dark, spotted skin. Regarded as the best of all the varieties of trout, it is served whole and can be grilled or baked. It can also be poached and served cold. Other trout cooked in the same way as the brown trout but not so superior are:

Grayling A silver-scaled fish belonging to the trout family.

Sea trout A migratory trout that feeds in fresh water and the sea. It is similar to a salmon with silver scales and pink flesh. Is always sold whole.

Sewin This is a sea trout, mostly caught in Wales between July and August. It weighs about 1lb (0.5kg).

Rainbow trout A common trout reared on fish farms. Is greenish-gold in colour with whitish flesh.

Smoked trout A rainbow trout that has been smoked to a rich brown colour. It requires no cooking and is served with a salad or as a starter.

SHELLFISH

The south-western beaches of Britain are rich in shellfish. These are either crustaceans such as crabs, lobsters and shrimps which have jointed shells; or molluscs such as mussels, oysters, scallops, etc which have hinged shells.

Clams

American mollusc now available in Britain. It is sold in its shell and served raw like oysters. Is also available smoked and tinned.

Cockles

Have a small oval shell in a golden greyish colour. They will cleanse themselves by removing sand if given a handful of flour and left overnight. They can then be boiled and as soon as they open they are done; but throw away the closed ones. They can also be baked and eaten hot.

Crabs

A crab is greyish brown when alive and brownish red when

cooked. It is sometimes sold alive. Kill it by dropping in boiling water and boiling briskly for 20 minutes. Do not allow it to cool in the water. You will then need some pliers and a hammer to break the shell and remove the flesh. To dress a crab, empty the shell and keep the coloured meat separate from the white. Then rearrange the meats in columns in the shell and garnish with cooked sieved egg yolk, chopped cooked egg white and parsley. The best crabs are heavy when held; small ones are usually watery. Crab also makes a good soup.

Crawfish

This is mostly caught off the south-west coast. It looks like a lobster without the large pincer claws and has very long horns and a butterfly tail. Is coarser in texture than lobster meat, but is prepared and cooked like a lobster. If you catch one, kill it by sticking a pointed knife through the spine behind the head. You can buy crawfish tails, as this is where most of the meat can be obtained.

Limpets

These are dome-shaped and greyish in colour. They can be prised off the rocks when the tide goes out, and used in the same way as cockles and mussels.

Lobsters

A crustacean that is a dark blue when alive and scarlet when boiled. The flesh of the male lobster, or cock lobster as it's called, is more delicate in flavour than the female or hen lobster. When boiling, especially the hen, tie the claws securely otherwise it will reach out and turn off the gas! Drop it in boiling water and boil for 15 to 20 minutes, then dry it and rub the shell with oil to give it a shine. Of course lobsters can be baked as well as boiled. When buying lobsters choose a heavy medium size one with a tail that springs back when it is straightened out. Avoid lobsters with white shells on their backs as this is a sign of age. It has a rich, nutritious flesh and needs condiments to accompany it.

Mussels

Common mussels are found all round the coast of Britain. They are usually 2in (5cm) in length and rectangular in shape. Colour is mostly dark blue or blackish, but can be brown or even yellow. They can be eaten raw but they must have come from an impeccable source. Eat the day they are gathered or keep them alive in salted water. Scrub the shell well to remove the 'beards'. Any broken shells or those that stay open when tapped should be thrown away. Cook them in water, or with wine added, for 5 to 10 minutes or until they open. They can also be baked. Mussels are often sold by the pint and a pint weighs approximately 1lb (0.5kg). They are delicious if served in a garlic and cream sauce.

Oysters
A large round, knobbly, greyish shell that hinges together. According to an old saying, oysters should only be eaten if there's a R in the month. They are very expensive and sold singly. They are eaten uncooked and swallowed whole. Can also be cooked, and used as a filling for steaks.

Periwinkles
This common little seashell is dark grey or reddish and sharply pointed. Periwinkles are never out of season but are at their best between September and April. Wash them well and boil for 20 minutes in salted water. You will need a pin to eat them.

Prawns
These are 1 to 4in (2.5–10cm) long, their transparent bodies dotted with purple pigment cells. Like other crustaceans they turn pink when boiled. They are the same shape as shrimps but much larger, and are eaten after they have been boiled. In their shells they are sold by the pint, but without their shells they are sold by weight. They can be used in curries, cocktails, soup, or served as a decoration on other dishes.

Razor fish
These have long, thin, golden-grey shells. They are best removed from their shells, boiled and eaten like other shell-fish.

Scallops
Fan-shaped shells coloured pinkish-brown. On opening the shell, trim away the beards and remove the black portion, leaving the yellowy-orange and white part of the fish. Remove this flesh and

wash well. Scrub the shells and replace the flesh. They can be eaten raw but are better baked or grilled in their shells with a sauce and breadcrumbs.

Shrimps
Small crustaceans with grey-brown soft shells that turn pink when boiled. They are usually sold boiled but, if you catch your own, boil them for 5 minutes. Served in soups, salads and as shrimp cocktails or eaten on their own.

Whelks
Are large and snail-shaped. Usually off-white in colour, but can be brown, yellow or pink. Gather only the medium-sized ones as the large ones can be tough. Clean them well in several changes of water. Cook them by dropping into boiling water, then take the pan off the heat or they will go rubbery. Allow to cool in the water for 1 to 1½ hours. There is a small hard piece at the end of the shell which must be removed. They make good fritters.

Winkles
The same as periwinkles.

10

Toss It in the Hay or Smoke It

Two very different methods of cooking are to use a hay box and to smoke food. Both are easier in the open—hopefully hay is easily available there and smoking is better done outdoors—but hay-box cooking is a good method of simmering food at home.

HAY-BOX COOKERY

Provided the camper has enough space, hay-box cookery is an excellent method. You might think this is an old-fashioned way of cooking, and so it is, but it's as effective today as it was when our grandmothers used it. In principle the idea is to make an insulated box in which you place a boiling pot and, by excluding the air, the food slowly cooks itself. It's so easy if you abide by a few rules.

First of all you need a good hay box. In order to make it you will need a large wooden box with a well-fitting lid. You can use a thick cardboard box, but this won't be so effective. Next, line the box well with several layers of paper, then make a pad or cushion that will fit inside the lid of the box and exclude any air. Fill the box with hay, packing it well into the corners, but allow enough space for the pot. There should be 4in (10cm) thickness of hay between the pot and the sides of the box. If the box is large enough you may be able to place more than one pot in it, but they must be well packed. The lid must be well secured and, if in doubt, cover the whole box with a blanket.

This is a very slow method of cooking so allow a good deal of time between preparation and eating. The idea is to heat the meal to boiling point and then quickly place it in the hay box and secure the lid well so that it continues to cook in its own heat. Gradually it will cool down and then it needs to be reheated before eating. This method can be slightly hurried up by half cooking the meal before placing it in the box. The advantages are that the meal will cook itself without constant stirring and supervision and one saves on fuel. There is no danger of overcooking. You can also heat your porridge at bed time and it's ready for you at breakfast. Once you have placed the pot in the box don't lift the lid to add another pot, as this will mean the heat is lost and the box is no longer effective. All items should be placed in the box at the same time.

It is easier to use billy-cans in a hay box rather than saucepans since there are no awkward handles. If the pans are slightly sooty then it's advisable to wrap them in newspaper before placing them in the box as this will keep the hay clean. The cooking time can be calculated by boiling the pot half the recommended time and then cooking in the hay box for three times as long as stated. Here is a guide to help you:

Bacon (boiled bacon)	45 minutes over heat; 3–4 hours or overnight in the box
Beans	Soak over-night, 1 hour over heat; 3 hours in the box
Boiled joint (beef, mutton, etc)	1 hour over heat; 4–5 hours in the box
Dried fruit	Soak over-night; 5–10 minutes over heat; 3–4 hours in the box
Fruit	All berries and fresh fruit need only be brought to the boil; 2 hours in the box
Porridge	2–3 minutes over heat; 4 hours or overnight in the box
Potatoes	5 minutes over heat; 2 hours in the box
Rice	5 minutes over heat; 1 hour in the box
Root vegetables	5–10 minutes over heat; 2 hours in the box
Soups	20–30 minutes over heat; 2 hours in the box
Stew	25 minutes over heat; 3–4 hours in the box
Tea or cocoa	Remove the tea leaves or bag first and then leave until required; it will not stew

If you haven't got a large box, you can still make a 'hay box' by making a hole in the ground and following the same rules. The hole can be lined with stones before adding the paper and hay.

Smoke cookery isn't something new. It has been a method of preservation since Neolithic times when man built fires and suspended his meat and fish above them. The method has not changed much except that the process is quicker, and brine is used as well. The principle of smoking is to have a fire lit under an oven so that the smoke from it penetrates through the oven, smoking the food that is suspended inside.

There are many ways of making a smoking oven, from a cardboard box to a large steel thermostatically controlled insulated oven. In order to keep it simple I shall give three ways of making a smoker.

If you are in the open you can make a pit-type smoker. To do this, dig a pit 2ft (0.6m) square and 2ft (0.6m) deep and a trench 9in (22cm) deep running downward from the pit. Light a pile of small smoky hardwood in the pit so that the wind forces the smoke along the trench and through the box. If the oven is made from cardboard the trench will need to be 3ft (1m) long; if using a wooden oven, 2ft (0.6m) long; and only 1ft (30m) long if using a metal oven. Next prepare the oven by punching small holes in the sides and placing sticks or wires through them on which to place or hang the fish or meat. Punch two holes in the top of the cardboard box for the smoke to escape. The box has no bottom as this is placed on the end of the trench. Cover the length of the trench with boards, foil, branches, etc; anything that will prevent the smoke from escaping. Long trenches cool the smoke, so the smoking process if a cardboard oven is used is longer, and will take up to 10 to 12 hours.

For campers there is an easier way. Cut 6 to 8 Y-shaped branches and half as many straight ones. Dig a small pit in the ground and stick the Y-shaped ones around it. Lay the other sticks horizontally on the crotches and hang the meat and fish from them. Build a small smoky fire in the pit and cover the whole structure with branches, canvas, plastic, etc; anything that will prevent the smoke from escaping. If you prefer not to dig a pit then make the fire in a bucket.

Besides making the smoker there are other rules one must observe.

Wood

Only use deciduous wood that bears leaves, and not conifers that produce needles. Therefore fir, spruce, pine and cedar are unsuitable. The smoke from these woods will give the food a nasty taste. If you wish you can light the fire from charcoal and then place sawdust or wood chips on top

Brine

Before placing the food in the smoker it has to be dipped in brine, or, more usually in the case of meat, in a pickle, a recipe for which is given overleaf. The brine for fish is made by adding 2lb 9oz (1.3kg) of salt to 1gal (4.5l) of cold water. As a test it should be strong enough to float an egg. During use the brine will lose its strength and it is a good idea to check with the egg, adding more salt when necessary. The length of soaking time will vary with the weight of fish. As a guide: under 4oz (115g), brine for 30 minutes; 8oz–1lb (225–455g), brine for 1 hour; 2–3lb (1–1.4kg), brine for 3 hours and so on. These are the times for white or non-oily fish. If using oily fish increase the brineing time by 25 per cent. Check with Chapter 9 for the types of fish.

Once the fish have been brined, wash them and allow them to dry before placing in the smoker. Times for smoking will vary with the type of oven, wood used and one's own personal taste, but an average of $1\frac{1}{2}$ to 2 hours should be a guide. When placing the fish in the oven make sure the smoke can circulate completely around each piece of fish otherwise there will be an uneven taste.

Several makes of smoke dust are commercially made and can be bought from a fishing-tackle shop. One can also buy an oven, but if you have an old biscuit tin it's easy to make one. In the bottom of the tin place 2 dessertspoonfuls of the dust. Place a small grill on top of the dust (one from a grill pan should fit) or cut one to size. Gut, wash and fillet the fish and don't use a brine, but sprinkle with a little salt and lay the fish on the rack. Put the lid on the tin and place the whole over a burner and heat for 2 to 3 minutes. Turn off the heat and allow to cool intact for 10 to 15 minutes. There is no need to make holes in the tin as most lids are not that tight fitting.

Pickle for Meat Using Briskets etc

Ingredients

1gal (4.5l) of water
¼oz (7g) saltpetre
1lb (455g) salt

1 to 2 crushed garlic cloves
4oz (115g) white sugar
1oz (30g) pickling spices

Method

Mix the solution and keep the meat submerged in it for 10 days if the pieces weigh between 2 and 4lb and longer according to weight. If the brine changes colour or smells sour throw it away and wash the meat well. It should be kept at a temperature of 1.7°C (35°F).

Sausages and burgers can be smoked. They don't need to be soaked in brine but have to be cooked before smoking.

It's advisable to find out, before starting any of this type of cooking, if fires may be lit on the site. Care should also be taken if camping in the wild so as not to cause a fire hazard.

11

Food Free for the Gathering

There are many wild plants, fruits and berries that are free just for the gathering. While one is camping in the countryside is an ideal time to look out for these. Not all vegetation, fungi or berries are fit for human consumption. There are comparatively few that are poisonous but, if in any doubt, don't pick them. There are 3,000 species of fungi and only 20-odd are not worth eating because they are tough or have an unpleasant taste, but of these 4 are fatal if eaten. While gathering free food don't take all the produce from one plant as this will weaken it. Look around and take a little from a few.

I am not giving a comprehensive list of all edible foods, but only those you will easily find. Many of the plants have various local names but I have used only the most common name. Shellfish are described in Chapter 9.

Berries

Barberry
Is found in hedgerows and bushy places. It has oval leaves and small yellow flowers. In July the oblong-shaped orange-red berries form in clusters. They can be baked or stewed. They make a good jam or jelly and are excellent served with cooked meats.

Bilberry or whortleberry
Is found mostly in woodlands and hedges. Is a low shrub with small bright-green leaves and grows amongst the heather. The berries can be picked from July to September. They can be eaten raw or with the addition of cream, and can also be stewed or made into pies and tarts. They are often known as 'blaeberries' or 'whorts'.

Blackberries
The fruit of the common bramble and found in most hedgerows in the British Isles. It's a prickly straggly plant with white or mauvish flowers. The fruit is red when first set and then turns to

a deep purple or black. The uses are numerous, from being eaten raw to stewed, made into pies and tarts, jam, and jelly. They also freeze very well.

Bullace
Often found in the hedgerows but not too common. Is the fore-runner of the domestic plum. It looks like a sloe but the fruit is more egg-shaped. Is acid but not so sour as the sloe and better eaten after a frost. Use stewed, or in pies and tarts or as a preserve.

Crab apples
The crab apple tree can be found in the hedgerows and is recog-nised by its irregular trunk and twisted reddish-brown branches. The apples are small and round in shape. They are yellowish-green but sometimes turn red and can be picked from July to December. They are not good to eat raw but can be cooked in the same way as apples and make an excellent jelly.

Cranberry
This plant is found in peaty bogs but, due to extensive drainage, is no longer so common. The berries are a mottled red and not good eaten raw, but make excellent tarts, pies and sauces.

Cloudberry
A very small shrub that doesn't grow more than 6in (15cm) high. It has a cluster of fruit at the end of the stem. The berries are bright orange and can be used in the same way as raspberries, but have a slightly apricot taste.

Dog rose
One of the rose family but the flowers are pink or white. The berries are scarlet and oval, unlike the rounded ones of the field rose. They are good eaten mashed and mixed with sugar and milk. They also make a good foundation for chutneys and jam.

Elderberry
This very common shrub is found on the sides of roads and in hedges. The berries are small, dark purple in colour, and grow in umbrella-shaped clusters. They can be picked from August to

October. The berries contain large pips and are not good eaten raw but make ideal tarts, preserves and wine.

Hawthorn berries

The most abundant berries in the autumn, and known as 'haws'. They are crimson in colour and spherical in shape; at one end of the berry is the remains of the flower. They hang in clusters and have a small stone inside them. They can be eaten raw with cream and sugar. They are excellent as a base for chutneys and jams. Their taste is said to resemble a sweet potato.

Juniper

An evergreen shrub that grows mostly on the moors and in the pinewoods of Scotland. The small green berries turn black in their second year when they are worth picking. They have the flavour of gin and are excellent in patés.

Redcurrant

Widespread in woods and hedgerows. The bush is 3–4ft (1–1.2m) in height. It resembles the cultivated currant bushes. The shiny red fruit, which has a translucent skin, is available in July.

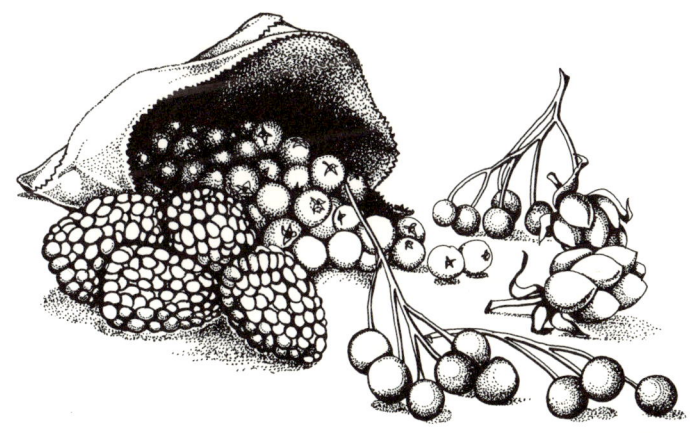

Rosehips

The fruit of the field rose. They are scarlet and spherical in shape, each one on its own stalk, with the remains of the withered flower at one end of the berry. The season is from late August to November. The berries are very sticky to the touch. They can be made into pies and tarts but the berry needs to be split and the pith and seeds removed before using. It makes an ideal syrup as it's rich in vitamin C.

Rowan

Fruit of the mountain ash. Bright orange-red in colour, they grow in clusters and are not true berries but small fruit. They are available from August to November. They make an excellent jelly to serve with meats.

Nuts

Beech

The tree is tall with a smooth grey bark. The nuts or seeds are found in a three-sided dark-brown, prickly husk. When the husk ripens it bursts and four three-sided brown nuts are shed. The shells can easily be peeled with one's fingers.

Hazel

This tree usually grows in hedgerows. Sometimes it never develops into a tree and resembles a shrub. During winter it produces long yellow, male catkins known as 'lamb's tails'. The nuts appear from September to October and are enclosed at the growing end with a small green foliage. The nuts can be collected in early autumn but are better eaten when the shell is brown.

Sweet chestnut

A tall, straight tree with single spear-shaped serrated leaves. Two or three chestnuts are found in a green prickly case. One must be careful not to mistake them for conkers, the fruit of the horse-chestnut, which are poisonous. The nuts are available in October and November and are superb if roasted over a fire. They can be eaten raw once the brown husk has been removed but are a little indigestible. They are excellent chopped and used in stuffings and vegetarian dishes.

Walnut

The trunk of the walnut tree is straight and silvery green, the leaves oblong in shape and bright green. The nut in late spring is enclosed in a soft green husk which turns black towards autumn. It usually falls off the tree enclosed in its black husk which rots on the ground and then the nut is visible. It is oval in shape with a light-brown, crinkly shell. Walnuts can be collected when light fawn in colour but are best kept and eaten when the shell is light brown. They can be eaten raw or used in salads, cakes, breads and various dishes, and are ideal for vegetarian cooking. Pickled walnuts are delicious served with cold meats. For this, collect the nuts when the green husk is still around them and they are tender enough to pass a needle through them. Place them in a brine for 9 days, then dry them in the sun for 4 days until they are very black and glisten. Next pack them into jars and cover with spiced vinegar.

Wild Herbs and Flavourings

Angelica

A tall plant with hollow stems and an umbrella-shaped cluster of pinkish flowers. The plant grows in both wet and grassy places. The leaves can be chopped and stewed with fruit, especially rhubarb. The stems make pretty decorations if candied.

Balm

A plant loved by bees. It has a long stem with pairs of leaves growing from it at regular intervals. The flower is white. The leaves are lemon scented and can be used in salads, stuffings, or dried and used as a tea.

Basil (wild)

A single stem plant with pairs of leaves growing from it. The vivid pink flowers grow beside the leaves. It is not an appetising plant but can be used in mushroom and tomato based dishes.

Borage

A very leafy plant with small blue flowers. Fresh leaves can be used in punches, and dried leaves as a tea.

Fennel

Found nearly everywhere. The plant grows to 5ft (1.5m) and has feathery leaves. The umbrella-shaped flowers have tiny yellow heads. Fennel has a strong aniseed flavour and is ideal if added when cooking oily fish. The stems can be dried and burnt as fuel when baking whole fish. It is good in salads.

Horseradish

Very common in England and Wales. The leaves are huge and look like dock leaves but grow straight from the stem to a height of 3ft (1m). The roots grow very deep and need a lot of digging out. They have to be scraped and this will make your eyes water. Then grate them and add them to cream or yoghourt and season well. Serve this sauce with roast beef or fish.

Lovage

This grows to 2ft (0.6m) tall and has bright leathery leaves and small white flowers. It has a strong celery taste. Leaves can be chopped and used to flavour stews and soups.

Marjoram

Often known as oregano, it is found on chalky and limestone soil, growing to 3ft (1m) in height. The leaves are oval with smooth edges and the flowers, which are a pale purple, appear at the top of the plant. This herb is excellent in casseroles, soups and in spaghetti sauces. Widely used in Mediterranean dishes. Very good dried.

Mint

Various types. *Common calamint* grows on grassy banks, particularly on chalk and limestone soil. It has the smell and flavour of a mixture of mint and marjoram. *Cornmint* is recognised by the smell of its green hairy leaves. Found nearly everywhere. Chop and add to vinegar.

Tansy

A plant with bright-yellow button type flowers on a long stalk. The leaves are ragged. They can be chopped and used in egg dishes, especially at Easter time. They have a slightly bitter taste.

Thyme

A small plant with very small dark-green leaves and purple flowers. Used as a flavouring in stuffings and meat dishes.

Salads and Vegetables

Burdock

Very common on roadsides and waste land. It has heart-shaped leaves and pink, thistle-type flowers. The young shoots should be picked in late spring and can be eaten in salads. The stems can be boiled in short lengths, once the outer peel has been stripped, and eaten like asparagus.

Chicory

Found on chalky soil. It has long ragged leaves like the dandelion and a small blue flower. The young leaves can be eaten as a salad. The roots can be roasted, ground and used as a substitute for coffee.

Chickweed

A gardeners' nightmare because it is so common. It has small bright-green leaves and small white flowers. The leaves can be made into a soup using a chicken base. They can also be chopped and sprinkled on salads.

Comfrey

Found near water. The plant grows to 3ft (1m) high and has dark-green spear-shaped leaves. The flowers appear from June to October and are white, mauve or pink. The leaves make excellent fritters if dipped in batter and deep-fried.

Dandelion

Found everywhere and easily identified by its large green ragged leaves that grow from its roots. The young leaves can be eaten in a salad. They can also be chopped and cooked like spinach. The root can be roasted and ground as a substitute for coffee.

Elderflower

The flower of the elder bush, creamy white and growing in umbrella-shaped clusters. Elderflowers are excellent as fritters if dipped in batter and then deep-fried. They also make a very good 'champagne', and give a 'lift' to all gooseberry dishes and jams.

Fat hen
A plant that grows to 3ft (1m) high, with diamond-shaped leaves and pale-green flowers. It can be eaten in the same way as cabbage and spinach.

Garlic (Jack-by-the-hedge)
Widespread, plentiful, and found on the edges of woods and by hedges. It has small white flowers and bright-green leaves. It smells of garlic and can be finely chopped and used in salads.

Ground elder
Widespread in hedges and shady places. It has finely toothed leaves that are grouped in threes at the end of the stalk. The flowers are white and in umbrella-shaped clusters. Cook the leaves as you would spinach.

Hawthorn
A shrub with ragged leaves and white or pink blossom. In autumn the berries are bright red. The shoot can be eaten in April and is sometimes known as 'bread and cheese', which is what the taste resembles. The leaves are also good in a salad.

Mallow
A common, bushy plant found by the roadsides, on waste places and by the sea. The flowers are a pretty purple colour and each has five petals. It flowers from June to October. The leaves can be cooked in the same way as spinach, and also make a good soup.

Nettle
A very common plant that grows everywhere. It's upright with a hairy stem and ragged leaves which 'sting' when touched. When cooked the sting is destroyed. Nettles should not be eaten after the end of May as the leaves become coarse and taste strong. They also act as a very powerful laxative if eaten at this time of the year. The two top shoots are the best to cook, either in a soup or treated like spinach. The leaves can also be made into a beer or tea. Use gloves when picking nettles.

Sea beet
Found on banks and shingle by the sea except in Scotland. It grows to 3ft (1m), and has large shiny leaves and tiny flowers that grow along its stem. The leaves can be picked from April to October. Strip the leaves from the central vein before tossing them in boiling water to cook. When tender drain well, and toss in butter.

Seaweeds
There are many seaweeds that are good to eat but I am only mentioning the two most popular. All are rich in minerals and need to be well washed in fresh water before use. *Carragheen, Irish moss* is purplish-brown in colour and its shape looks like the branches of a dying tree. It is full of vegetable gelatine and is used for thickening soups, stews, etc. *Laver* is common all around Britain. It has large, purple cabbage-shaped leaves, but appears very thin in texture and the veins are easily visible. Laver is very popular in Wales and is sold puréed and called laverbread. It is then rolled in oatmeal and fried with bacon.

Sorrel
Widely found, especially on acid soils, growing to 2ft (0.6m) with arrow-shaped leaves. It blooms from May to August, and has small red and green flowers. The leaves can be picked in early spring and eaten raw, but have an acid taste. They can be cooked like spinach but can also be chopped and used in soups.

Watercress
Must only be picked in fast-running water and then care must be taken to see that it's pure and clean. The leaves are small, bright green, and grow in bunches; the small white flower can be seen from June to October. It is exceptionally high in vitamin C. Best eaten raw, but also makes a good soup. When picking, cut pieces off rather than pull up the root.

Wild parsnip
Found in the south and east of England on chalk and limestone soil. It grows to 15in (0.4m) high and the yellow flowers appear on the top of the stalk as spokes on a wheel. It could be confused with fennel. The root of the wild parsnip has a stronger flavour

than that of the cultivated one. To prepare the roots, wash them well and then peel off the skin. Boil in water until soft and then sieve to remove tough fibres. The purée can then be used. Parsnips can also be boiled and eaten as a vegetable, but the centre core is inedible.

Mushroom and Other Fungi

There are so many kinds of edible fungi that it would be difficult to list them all so I have chosen those that are commonly found and easily recognisable. If they are not listed it doesn't mean they are not worth eating, and I suggest you get a good illustrated reference book to help you find these delicious morsels while wandering through the fields and woodlands.

Blewits
Can be found in grasslands and mostly grow in groups or rings. They look like the common mushroom but have wavy caps and bluish stalks. There is also a wood blewit that grows mostly in woodlands. All parts are lilac but the caps later turn reddish-brown. The lilac gills contain a substance that poisons the red blood cells but this is destroyed when cooked. They can be cooked by stewing them in milk with bacon and onion, then removing the fungi and making the liquor into a white sauce. Not a fungus to eat unless well cooked.

Field mushrooms
Available from August to November. The cap is white and the gills pink, gradually turning to brown. One should be able to peel the skin off the cap. They seem to appear overnight and, if lucky and up early enough in the morning, one can collect bucketfuls. It is best to cut them rather than pick them because then one doesn't disturb the spawn at the base. Most people over-cook mushrooms—they only need a few minutes sautéing in a little butter or fat. They also freeze well if first sautéd in fat or butter. They can enhance many dishes, make a good soup and can be eaten raw in salads.

Horse mushrooms
Very like the field mushroom but much larger in size—can grow

to 10in (25cm) in diameter. The gills are greyish and these mush-rooms often grow in rings. Because of their size they are excellent stuffed and baked. Otherwise slice them and use them as you would field mushrooms.

Puff ball
The puff ball is easily recognisable because it looks like a cream ball and can grow as large as a man's head. It has no stalk and grows straight from the ground. Puff balls must be eaten when young and white; forget them if they are creamy or fawn coloured.

Rabbits, Hares and Other Game

These are not usually free, but can often be bought very cheaply if you find the right source. I must emphasise that one cannot shoot for game and rabbits just where one wishes. Permission must be sought beforehand, as often the shooting rights have been sold. Any other method of catching rabbits, etc, such as snaring, is completely out of the question and mustn't even be considered. If you are staying on a small farmer's site and ask him for a rabbit if he has the time, he more than likely will shoot one for you. He might have a supply of rabbits from a good day's ferreting.

Markets often have rabbits and hares with their jackets on and many people are put off because they feel they couldn't tackle such a job as skinning. I assure you it's very easy and only like removing a tight glove. Most rabbits have had their innards removed and you can see the condition of the rabbit from examin-ing the inside which should look fresh and pinkish. Why pay double the price for a frozen thing when there's a first-rate rabbit full of flavour which only needs its jacket removed. If you are squeamish about drawing birds, wear a rubber glove the first few times and, after a while, you won't bother with the glove. Rabbits can be cooked in the same way as chicken. If you wish to get rid of some of the strong rabbit taste, soak it in salty water.

Skinning a rabbit
The innards should be removed shortly after being killed. To do this you need to make a slit from the end of the rib cage to the tail—taking care not to puncture the intestines—and tip out all the unwanted gut. You will find this comes away quite easily.

1 Take off all the feet. Dislocate the bottom joints by bending backwards and then cut them off.

2 Make a slit in the skin up the back of both the hind legs right up to the tail and peel off the skin. Ease the shin over the rump of the rabbit and cut off the tail.

3 Hold on to the naked back legs with one hand and the skin with the other and pull; you will find the skin comes off the back very easily.

4 Push the front legs up through the skin and cut through the neck. You should now be left with one piece of fur attached to the head; this you rip off.

4 Wash the meat well and it's ready for cooking. It can be jointed and it's best to remove the thin skin on its belly.

Hares can be skinned in the same way.

Pheasants and partridges

Limited season from September to February. They are better if allowed to hang with their innards in as then they have more flavour. Draw them before cooking. Can be roasted, or jointed and sautéd, or served in a sauce.

Woodcock

Are not hung like other game birds. They are not drawn before cooking. Best baked on a piece of fried bread to catch the juices.

Snipe

A very small bird that is not drawn before cooking. It should be cooked as soon as it's shot by baking or sautéing.

Pigeon

The breast is the best part and can be cut off the carcase. Very dry when being cooked and needs a little fat or bacon. Good cooked in wine or sautéd.

Wild duck

Much meatier than the domestic duck but not as greasy. They are drawn and roasted or casseroled.

Teal

A very small member of the duck family. Cooked in the same way.

When 'roasted' is mentioned it doesn't only mean cooked in an oven; one can also pot roast. This is done by using a heavy pan and melting enough fat in it to cover the base. Place the meat in it and brown over a high heat. Lift out the meat and place some vegetables or a wire rack in the pot; replace the meat on rack or vegetables. Cover with a well-fitting lid and cook over a low heat until meat is tender. Allow 45 minutes per lb and turn the meat while cooking.

12
Regional Dishes

The British produce some of the best foodstuffs in the world and therefore there is a wealth of dishes peculiar to these islands. On the whole British cookery is simple, as the ingredients themselves are so superb that they do not need spices and sauces to liven up the flavour. Besides giving dishes that are traditional in certain areas, I have given a list of local specialities. I don't intend you to cook all these delights yourself but look out for them on sale in shops, restaurants and markets. There is nothing worse than going on holiday only to find, when you return home again, that you haven't sampled the local delicacies.

To make life easier I have divided the British Isles into regions.

ENGLAND

Cumbria

Mutton Pies Small pies made from savoury shortcrust pastry and filled with minced lamb and herbs.

Cumberland Rum Nicky A tart filled with a mixture of dates, butter, ginger, and flavoured with rum.

Cumberland Sausage A port sausage made into 12in long links and twisted in a spiral. It is cut into portions after cooking.

Clipping-time Pudding A rice pudding flavoured with cinnamon, that has had dried fruit and beef marrow added to it.

Kendal Mint Cake A very thin peppermint cake made from sugar and milk. It is white or brown depending on the colour of the sugar used.

Westmorland Herb Pudding A boiled pudding containing young nettle tops, cabbage, bistort and barley and the leaves from the raspberry, gooseberry, dandelion and dock. It is served as a main course or as a vegetable with lamb.

Look out for: Lyth Valley damsons, Solway salmon, Herdwick lamb and Cumberland ham.

Northumbria

Felton Spice Loaf A fruit cake containing peel, almonds and mixed fruit.

South Tyne Yeast Cake A teabread containing mixed dried fruit.

Mitton of Pork A kind of pork terrine served hot with mushrooms and gravy, or cold with a salad.

Leek Pudding Suet pudding filled with chopped leeks.

Newcastle Pudding A steamed bread and butter pudding with a lemon flavour instead of dried fruit.

Panjotheram A casserole of chops and potatoes.

Singin' Hinnies A griddle cake containing fruit that, after it is cooked, is halved and buttered together.

Alnwick Stew A layered stew of bacon and potatoes.

Pan Haggerty A layered pie cooked in a frying pan and browned under a grill.

Northumbrian Aniseed Cake A cake made with honey and aniseed.

Bishop Auckland Cheesecake Small tarts filled with fruit and mashed potato, flavoured with lemon and rum.

Border Tarts Tartlets filled with almonds, finished with a trellis design and iced while warm.

Durham Fluffin A pudding made from barley, milk, nutmeg, sugar and brandy.

Look out for: Snabdough ginger bread; Berwick cockles; Cotherstone cheese; Lindisfarne mead, liqueur and fudge; and pease pudding.

North West

Tripe and Onions Tripe cooked in a creamy onion sauce.

Chorley Cakes Flat pastry-based cakes with currants.

Lancashire Hot Pot A stew or casserole of lamb or mutton chops, layered with potato and kidneys. Usually served in a brown pottery pot.

Potted Shrimps Shrimps mostly from Morecambe Bay, mixed with spices and potted with clarified butter.

Black Pudding A thick black sausage usually shaped in a circle. It is made from fresh pig's blood and a mixture of cereals and spices. To serve, heat the pudding in hot water for 10 to 15 minutes, or fry.

Eccles Cakes Round flat cakes, made from puff pastry, containing mixed dried fruit. They have two slits on the top.

Wet Nelly A pudding originally made from bread crusts left over from making bread sauce. Now the bread is crumbed and soaked in water and then baked. Spices are added.

Chester Pudding A steamed pudding containing blackcurrant jam and served with a blackcurrant sauce.

Look out for: Everton toffee, Bury simnel cakes, Derbyshire oat cakes, Goosnargh cakes and Soul Mass cakes.

Yorkshire and Humberside

Fat Rascals A homemade biscuit.

Courting Cake (Batley Cake) A large jam tart.

Curd Tarts Small tarts filled with curds and currants.

Beef Sausages Longer than those found elsewhere in the British Isles.

Yorkshire Veal and Oyster Oysters were once plentiful but now this is an expensive dish. Pieces of veal stuffed with oysters and coated with breadcrumbs, served in an oyster-flavoured gravy.

Yorkshire Christmas Pie Huge pies that were served at Christmas time. They were made from hot water pastry and filled with goose, forcemeat, pigeon, hare and tongue.

Yorkshire Pudding A light batter pudding served with roast beef.

Look out for: Pomfret cakes, Wensleydale cheese and Brontë liqueur.

Heart of England

Oldbury Tarts Small tartlets filled with gooseberries and brown sugar. The pastry is made from hot-water crust.

Fidget Pie Its name is derived from 'fitched', meaning five-sided and relating to the original shape of the pie. Is a layered baked pie consisting of bacon, apples and onion in a savoury shortcrust.

Shrewsbury Biscuits Biscuits made into $1\frac{1}{2}$in (3.7cm) rounds and containing caraway seeds.

Speech House Pudding Speciality from the Forest of Dean. It is a steamed pudding that has a marbled effect from the jam added to the mixture.

Love in Disguise   Calves' hearts stuffed with forcemeat, wrapped in bacon, covered in vermicelli and then roasted.

Malvern Pudding   A baked pudding with layers of batter and spiced apple.

Look out for: Double Gloucester cheese, lampreys and Malvern water.

Midlands

Quorn Bacon Roll   A round steamed pudding containing bacon, onion and sage. It was served to the beaters after a hunt meeting.

Belvoir Castle Buns   Round buns with alternate rings of dried fruit and yeast mixture.

Nottingham Pudding   The Bramley apple first came from South-well, Nottinghamshire. This is a baked pie of apples in a batter mixture.

Gotham Pudding   A steamed batter pudding served with cowslip wine.

Bosworth Jumbles   Biscuits made by King Richard III's cook on the battlefied of Bosworth.

Melton Mowbray Pork Pie   A raised pork pie.

Market Harborough Pork Pie   A pork pie layered with apples and onion.

Bakewell Tart   A sweet shortcrust tart filled with ground almonds and a layer of jam.

Look out for: Colwick cheese, Melton Hunt cake, Stilton cheese, Red Leicester cheese, Derby Sage cheese and Derbyshire oat-cakes.

Thames and Chilterns

Oxford Sausage   A sausage made from equal amounts of veal and pork. The mixture was not stuffed into skins but fried in cylindrical shapes.

Tandra Cake   A dried-fruit teabread.

Brown Betty   A nightcap made from brown ale and spices with a piece of toast floating on the top.

Grassy Corner Pudding   A cold dessert. It is shaped in a mould and consists of alternate layers of custard and strawberry-fruit cream.

Aylesbury Game Pie   A terrine made from a hare, chicken, a pheasant, veal, pork and herbs. It is usually served hot, but sometimes cold at a buffet.

New College Pudding Small balls of pudding made from suet, breadcrumbs, dried fruit, and flavoured with brandy. These puddings are then fried in hot butter.

Cherry Bumpers Served at the end of the cherry season. A tart filled with black cherries.

Brown Windsor Soup A thick brown soup that has madeira added just before serving.

Oxford Pudding A steamed pudding with a filling of pork, liver, bacon, onions, chestnuts and baked beans.

Look out for: Banbury cakes, Oxford marmalade, Hollygog pudding and Bosley bangers (sausages).

East Anglia

Suffolk Rusks Small bread rolls that have been sweetened after being baked.

Trinity Pudding A favourite sweet served at Trinity College (Cambridge). It is a rich creamed custard with a caramel topping. Also called Burnt Cream.

Fourses Cake A teabread made from dried fruit and spices.

Pig's Fry The Norfolk name for dumplings.

Ipswich Almond Pudding A rich custard over a base made from puff pastry.

Biffins Sweet apples that were dried in the oven until they were wrinkled. A dish called Black Caps was made using these apple rings baked in a sweet wine.

Look out for: Colchester oysters, samphire and Yarmouth bloaters.

London

Chelsea Buns Small buns made from dough and filled with dried fruit and spices. They are round and have rings of fruit and dough with a sugary top.

Richmond Maids of Honour Small tarts filled with curds, potatoes, almonds and spices.

Green Pea Soup A thick green pea soup with bacon, lentils and other vegetables added. It was sold hot from street barrows.

Eel and Mash   Hot eels in a parsley broth served by barrow boys with mashed potato.

East Ham Eel Pie   Jellied eels in a pastry crust.

Look out for: Jellied eels, London buns and boiled beef and carrots.

West Country

Bath Buns   Buns made from a rich dough with grated lump sugar sprinkled on top.

Lardy Cakes   Rich dough with dried fruit and spices that has a very high quantity of lard added. It is very greasy and should be broken and not cut when serving.

Saffron Cakes   A teabread made with dried fruit and flavoured with saffron. It is bright yellow in colour. A speciality of Cornwall.

Sally Lunn Buns   A large rich tea bun that, after it has been cooked, is toasted and filled with cream and jam. They were named after Sally Lunn who used to sell them in the streets.

Fairings   A biscuit made from a rich mixture flavoured with ginger. They were sold at fairs.

Cornish Pasty   A pasty filled with meat and vegetables. Sometimes called a 'tiddy oggy'.

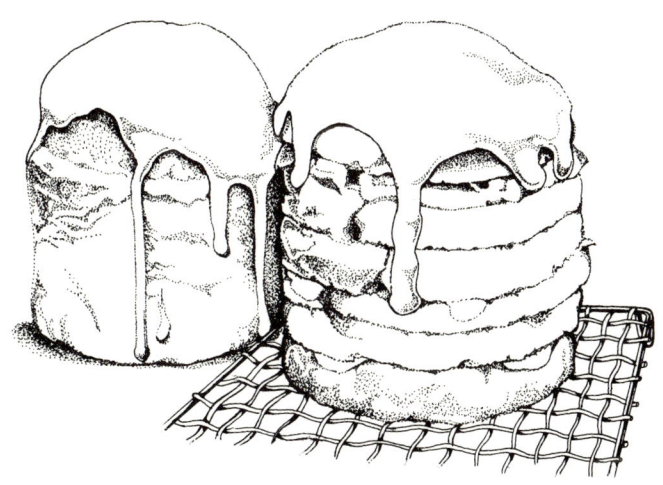

Squab Pie   A baked pie containing lamb chops, apples and onions topped with a pastry lid. Originally the lamb was replaced with young pigeons.

Star-gazy Pie   A pastry pie made from pilchards, bacon and chopped egg. The finished dish has the heads of the fish poking out of the hole in the middle.

Elvers   Young eels that are caught in the spring. They are blanched in hot water and then drained and made into an omelette.

Look out for: Cider, Ilchester cheese, Mendip snails, Bath Olivers (biscuits), clotted cream, chudleighs, Dorset knobs, Bath chap and polonies, Dorset Blue cheese, and farmhouse Cheddar.

South East

Pulborough Eels   Steamed pudding containing eels, pickled pork, hard-boiled eggs and vegetables.

Arundel Mullets   A fish soup that is poured over a piece of bread.

Chichester Pudding   A baked pie that has a rich custard, frothed with egg whites, over a breadcrumb base.

Oast Cakes   Small cakes made from a dough mixture and fried in fat until golden.

Plum Duff   A steamed pudding cooked in a cloth. The pudding contains dried fruit and is served with a melted redcurrant sauce.

Look out for: Variety of shellfish, Dover sole, cherries.

Southern

Hampshire Pie   A shortcrust tart containing a filling made from eggs, jam and butter.

Gingerbread Husbands   A gingerbread dough pressed into moulds and sold at fairs.

Isle of Wight Pies   Small tarts filled with eggs, sugar, nutmeg and rice with half a cherry placed on top.

Look out for: Wine from Hambledon and Beaulieu, and venison.

SCOTLAND

Cock-a-Leekie   A soup made from leeks and onions with pieces of chicken added before serving.

Cullen Skink   A fish broth made from Finnan haddock, potatoes and onion.

Scotch Broth   A good thick soup made from various vegetables and thickened with barley.

Kilkenny Kail   A soup made from rabbit, bacon and kail (greens).

Tweed Kettle   Poached salmon in a wine and onion liquor.

Haggis and Neeps   Haggis is a sheep's stomach filled with oatmeal, suet, onions and herbs. Neeps are mashed turnip, served hot with the haggis.

Forfar Bridies   These are semi-circular pasties filled with chopped beef, suet and flavourings.

Clapshot   A vegetable dish made from potatoes, turnips, chives and butter.

Rumbledethumps   A dish that has been grilled and contains cabbage, mashed potatoes and onions.

Skirlie   A dish made from oatmeal, onions and suet that is fried and eaten as an accompaniment to meat.

Stovies   An old Scottish vegetable dish of sliced potato and onion served alone or with cold meat.

Colcannon   A mixture of cooked vegetables in a brown stock.

Pitcaithly Bannocks   Large round biscuits flavoured with lemon peel and almonds, with caraway seeds and peel on the top.

Look out for: Arbroath smokies, Finnan haddock, kippers, shortbread, oatcakes, whisky and its products.

IRELAND

Coddle   A layered stew of bacon, potatoes, sausages and onions served from the pot it was cooked it. It is always served very hot.

Carragheen Moss   An edible seaweed. It is gathered in spring and preserved by the sun. When dried it is known as Irish Moss. Various dishes are made from it, including Carragheen Moss Chocolate Soufflé, Carrageen Moss Fruit Mould, and Lemon Soufflé.

Duileasc   Edible seaweed.

Sleabha   Edible seaweed.

Boxty Bread Irish potato dish served on the eve of All Saint's Day. It's a griddle cake shaped into large flat rounds that split into four. The ingredients used were mashed and uncooked potato, flour and bacon fat.

Dippity Bread An oat bread made with milk.

Beef Braised with Onions, Carrots and Guinness A casserole, often including prunes stuffed with hazel nuts.

Brown Bread A soda bread using wholemeal flour.

Barmbrack A bread made with yeast but shaped in rounds. It contains dried fruit and has a sticky sugar top. It's best served warm with butter.

Irish Mist Coffee A strong glass of coffee with cream floating on the top with the addition of Irish Mist liqueur.

Drisheens A steamed pudding made from sheep's blood, suet, breadcrumbs and herbs.

Nettle Pottage A thick soup made from young nettles and thickened with oatmeal.

Pratie Apple Cake A dough made from mashed cooked potatoes and flour, with a layer of applies in between. Sugar or honey is added to the top.

Look out for: Caca Cleamhnais, various fish, bacon, Guinness, Irish whiskey and champ.

WALES

Pice ar y Maen (Welsh Cakes) Round small scones containing currants and spices, cooked on a griddle and best served hot.

Grempog (Welsh pancakes) Pancakes made with soda and cream of tartar.

Bara Brith (Speckled Bread) Traditionally a fruit bread made from yeast, but not using self-raising flour.

Bara Lawr Wyau a Chig Moch Laver bread and oatmeal served with egg and bacon.

Gaws Pobi (Welsh Rarebit) Grated cheese with beer, mustard and Worcester sauce mixed together and then placed on toast and grilled.

Pastai Gocos (Cockle Pie) A tart filled with layers of cockles, onions and bacon, with a lattice pattern on the top.

Cawl Cennin (Leek Broth) Thick soup containing leeks, bacon and other vegetables, and thickened with oatmeal.

Pastai Persli (Parsley Pie) A pastry tart filled with chopped parsley, eggs and bacon.

Ff est y Cybydd (Miser's Feast) A pot containing boiled potatoes with an onion added. When cooked, slices of ham or bacon are added to the pot and it's allowed to cook until all the water has been absorbed.

Brithyll a Chig Moch (Trout and Bacon) Trout stuffed with herbs and wrapped in a rasher of bacon. Mud used to be used instead of bacon.

Enllyn Bara Lawr ac Oen Cymreig (Lamb and Laverbread Roll) Stuffed loin of lamb, roasted and then wrapped in pastry.

Cacen Ddu Patagonia A very rich fruit cake with a sugary top.

Berffro Cakes Small cakes that are often marked with a scallop shell.

Troliod (Trollins) Small rounds of dumplings that are served as a sweet with demerara sugar and butter.

Look out for: Homemade produce, sewin, trout, Welsh lamb, laverbread, laver (sold as a purée, red variety considered superior to the green), fresh fish and vegetables. Welsh markets are full of goodies and should not be missed.

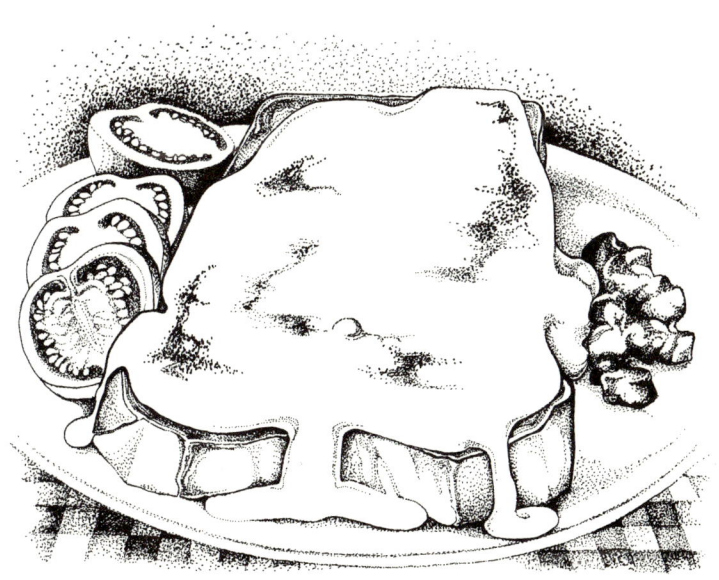

13
Food That Will Travel

If you have enough space it's a good idea to make and bake some items that will travel on holiday with you. Some will keep for a week or two, but remember cooked meats and pies do not keep, especially in warm weather. It's amazing how hungry the open air makes the family feel and these items provide them with some good 'nibbles' between meals. I like to take a cooked chicken or roasted meat with me to eat en route, or for that first meal on the site as then it needs little preparation after travelling. Most of the recipes you will find somewhere in your cookery books, but the more elusive are given here for easy reference.

ITEMS TO TAKE WITH YOU

Large fruit cake or luncheon cake   These will keep well in a tin or plastic bag.

Pastry cases   Line the case with foil and leave in the tin it's been cooked in and then there's less chance of it breaking. On the site fill with sweet or savoury fillings.

Meringues   Take small ones rather than large rounds as they won't break so easily. Pack in airtight containers or plastic bags. They can be used later by sandwiching together with fresh cream, or served with ice cream, fruit salads, etc.

Digestive biscuits   Can be used in the same way as brown bread, but delicious on their own or with cheese, or crumbled as a pastry base.

Shrewsbury biscuits   A sweet biscuit.

Flapjack   An oatmeal biscuit that can be served on its own or crumbled to make a base to a sweet.

Brandy snaps   Very brittle. Store in airtight containers; can be filled with cream just before use.

Gingerbread   Improves with keeping.

Gingerbread men   Ginger biscuits shaped in the form of men.

Victoria sandwich or sponge   Better to keep them with no fillings.

Vinaigrette dressing   Keep in an airtight jar or bottle.

Homemade squash   Keep well screwed down when not in use.

Digestive Biscuits

Ingredients

3oz (85g) butter or margarine
4oz (115g) wholemeal flour
4oz (115g) medium sized
  oatmeal
2oz (55g) castor sugar

pinch of salt
small pinch of bicarbonate
  of soda
½ egg

Method

1 Rub the fat into the flour and add all the dry ingredients, mixing well. Bind with the beaten egg.
2 Roll out and cut into small shapes. Place on a greased baking tray and cook for 5 to 8 minutes in an oven 375°F (190°C) or Gas 6.
3 Cool on a wire tray.

Shrewsbury Biscuits

Ingredients

4oz (115g) butter
4oz (115g) castor sugar
1 large egg
8oz (225g) plain flour

pinch of salt
1 level tsp grated lemon
  rind

Method

1 Cream the butter and sugar and add the beaten egg a little at a time.
2 Mix the flour, salt and rind into the mixture. If too soft, place in the fridge for 20 minutes.
3 On a lightly floured surface roll out to ⅛in thickness. Cut into rounds.
4 Place on a greased baking tray and cook in an oven 350°F (177°C) or Gas 4 for 15 minutes.
5 Remove from baking tray, cool on a wire tray and dredge with castor sugar.

Flapjack

Ingredients

3oz (85g) brown sugar,
preferably soft
1 dessertspoon syrup
3oz (85g) margarine

4oz (115g) oats
½ level tsp ginger
pinch of salt

Method

1 Melt the sugar, syrup and margarine in a saucepan, add oats, ginger and salt. Stir well.
2 Press down well in a greased tin and cook for 15 to 20 minutes in an oven 375°F (190°C) or Gas 5.
3 Mark the flapjack after it has left the oven and allow to cool in the tin.

Gingerbread

Ingredients

2oz (55g) lard
2oz (55g) brown sugar
4oz (115g) treacle
¼pt (150ml) milk

8oz (225g) plain flour
¼tsp salt
2 level tsp ground ginger
½tsp bicarbonate of soda

Method

1 Warm the fat, sugar and treacle in a pan until the fat has melted. Add the sifted flour, salt, ginger and bicarbonate of soda. Mix well.
2 Place in a greased 6in (15cm) square tin and cook in an oven 350°F (177°C) or Gas 4 for 1½ to 2 hours. The cake should not be cut for 24 hours.

Gingerbread Men

Ingredients

10oz (285g) self-raising flour	3oz (85g) butter
4oz (115g) castor sugar	3tbs golden syrup
4 level tsp ground ginger	1tsp black treacle
1½tsp cinnamon	1 beaten egg

Method

1 Blend all the dry ingredients together. Rub in the butter. Add syrup and treacle and mix well. Add the egg and mix again.
2 Roll out onto a floured surface and cut into figure shapes. If too sticky place the mixture in the fridge for a while.
3 Make features with currants and pieces of cherry. Cook in an oven 250°F (121°C) or Gas 1 for 45 minutes to 1 hour.
4 Cool on a wire tray.

Brandy Snaps

Ingredients
- 2oz (55g) butter
- 2oz (55g) sugar
- 2oz (55g) golden syrup
- 2oz (55g) plain flour
- $\frac{1}{2}$tsp ground ginger
- 1tsp brandy

Method
1 Melt the fat with the sugar and the syrup in a pan. Add the flour, ginger and brandy.
2 Grease a baking tray and place a teaspoon of the mixture on it, allowing 3 to 4in (8–10cm) for spreading.
3 Bake for 8 to 10 minutes in an oven 325–350°F (163–177°C) or Gas 3–4.
4 Remove from baking tray and allow to cool a little before rolling around the handle of a greased wooden spoon. Cool on a wire tray.

Homemade Squash

Ingredients
- 2 lemons
- 2 oranges
- 2pt (1l) water
- 6oz (170g) sugar
- 1oz citric acid

Method
1 Peel the skin off the fruit without cutting the pith, and boil in water until soft (approximately 15 minutes).
2 Add the sugar and acid, making sure they are dissolved. Place in a liquidiser and blend for 10 seconds.
3 Strain the mixture and add the juice that has been squeezed from the fruit.
4 Place in a bottle and dilute with water or soda.

Index